Who's Up?

Who's Up?

IS A SALES CAREER RIGHT FOR YOU?

A Sales Book

Robert F. Dieterich

ISBN: 1508528357
ISBN 13: 9781508528357
Library of Congress Control Number: 2015918624
CreateSpace Independent Publishing Platform
North Charleston, South Carolina

Contents

Preface

You are beginning a book that could change your life. No matter what you are doing now to earn a living or just to keep busy, you should read this book and ask yourself if this sounds like a better career than the one you have now.

I wrote this book for people who want to know more about a sales career and if it might be right for them. Additionally, if you are currently a salesperson or if you just wonder, what sales are all about; this book will help you and maybe even change your life. I have included in this book everything a salesperson or a buyer needs to know.

With this book in your library, you will not need any other sales books. This one covers it all, from A to Z.

About the Title

The phrase "Who's Up" was a very important part of my life every day.

At the local Chevy dealer where I started my sales career, whoever spotted a prospect first would yell, "Who's up?" when a prospect came onto the lot or entered the showroom. That phrase meant whose turn is it to approach and talk to the next prospect?

We took turns based on who came in first in the morning, then who came in second, and so on. Generally, five salespeople worked a shift. If you got in late, you could go all day without an "up" (a prospect to talk to).

This routine became so engrained in my life that I sometimes woke up yelling, "Who's up?" I heard this many times every day for the ten years I worked there.

About Bob Dieterich

At the time of writing, I am seventy-one years old. I started in sales at the age of twenty-four. At that time, I was working as an operations manager for a large stock-brokerage firm. I loved this job but could only make about $5,500.00 a year. I had a wife, two beautiful kids, and a very small, comfortable home with a mortgage that took 35 percent of my pay. With other bills and living expenses, I had no money to afford a new or even a late model used car. I wanted one very badly; before I got married at the age of twenty-one, I purchased a new car every year. It was the most important thing in the world to me until I got married and had a family.

I had never thought about being a salesperson, but an ad in my local newspaper for a new-car salesperson caught my eye because a new car would be provided to salespeople every six months along with gas, insurance, and all maintenance. *Wow!* I could not believe it. A free car and all expenses—this was my dream job. I figured any dope could sell cars. This was the perfect job for me. I interviewed for the job, and the manager said I was nuts for wanting the job because I had a better job at that time. I said I did not care; all I wanted to do was sell cars. (By the way, if I get the job, when do I get my new car?) I interviewed three times for the job and finally landed the position of a new-car salesman. I rushed home and told my wife that we were getting a new car. I was not that excited about getting the job, only the new car.

I swear to you right now that the only reason I wanted that job was for the car.

Well, when I showed up for work, I had on a brand-new suit (back then, salesmen wore suits and ties), and I sat in the manager's office and asked him about their training program. He said, OK, here it is. This is your price book; over three hundred cars are out on the lot, and here comes your first customer. Good luck. Within two weeks, I had sold a lot. I sold my stereo, my TV, and anything else I could sell to get some money to live on. I had not sold a single car. My aunt was thinking about buying a car from me but decided to shop around to see if she could get a better deal.

My boss called me into his office and said that I was doing terribly. Let me give you some advice, he said. He had previously told me that if I ever needed help to let him know. I thought now he was going to give me all the wisdom of his many years in the car business.

What he said was "If you don't start selling a lot more cars you are fired." Plain and simple: I would be fired. Instead of thinking about how I could support my family, the only thing that I could think about was losing my beautiful new car. I was not about to let that happen.

I had finally figured out that the company could not care less about me; it only cared about how many cars I could sell. It had no training program at all, and it would just keep hiring salespeople until it got one that could sell. If it had to go through twenty salespeople to get one, that would have been just fine.

Armed with the fear of losing my new car, I decided that if I was going to learn how to sell then I was going to have to teach myself. I did several things that helped me out.

How I started out:

1. First, I decided to listen to the things the other salespeople were saying to prospects that ended up buying. I would make notes and start using those things.
2. Next, I made a list of things that the bad salespeople were saying to prospects that actually killed any chance of making a sale.
3. I made a list of things I saw people liked and things they did not like. The good things I would say and the bad things I would avoid.
4. I bought many books on sales, but I was frustrated with them because they all had general concepts about sales. What I really wanted was someone to give me the exact words to say to sell the car. None of the books on the market had this.
5. Next, I decided to use all the existing tools I had at my disposal to help sell the car, such as my great personality and my energy (I was only twenty-four and willing to work hard). I made friends with the successful salespeople and spent a lot of time with them. None of them really wanted to see me get better, as it would make them look bad. However, when asked, their big egos just could not let them not give me a good answer.

Well, before long all these things made a difference. Within three months, I was the number three salesperson out of fifteen that worked at the dealership. At least at this point, my job was secure.

I was thrilled with my new car but noticed that some salespeople had better cars than I had. One day, I asked the manager why some guys had better cars. (All I had was a car with power steering, power brakes, a standard radio, a vinyl top, and a great set of wheels.) One person there even got to order his own demo, and he loaded it up with every option you could get.

The manager said that the guys with the most seniority or the guys who sold the most cars got to pick out anything they wanted to drive or even order the car themselves if there was nothing on the lot that they liked. Well, this was all I needed to hear to decide that I was going to drive a new Chevrolet Corvette. (We were a Chevy dealer.) I had developed some good skills and was now on track to earn about $13,000.00 my first year plus a new car and gas. I was making more money than any of my friends were (at almost triple the pay I had been making at my old job).

However, since there was not anything I could do about the seniority thing to get my Corvette, all I could do was be the top salesperson. While I learned a lot and was doing well, I realized that I could not be the top salesperson at the dealership without some more help. I asked my manager if I could attend some sales seminars to improve my selling skills. He said I could have some time off to attend the seminars, but I would have to pay for them myself.

While I did not like this deal, I took it anyway in order to get my new Corvette. I signed up for as many sales seminars as I could afford, thinking this would be the answer to more sales. I found that none of the seminars could significantly improve the skills that I had developed myself, but I did note that I could always bring home one good, useful thing. It took a long time and many seminars, but I was building a written log of all the good things I could use. My sales started to go up slowly but surely.

One day it dawned on me that if I could learn one good thing from an otherwise lousy seminar, maybe I could learn one good thing from the bad salespeople whom I knew were going to be fired. I started listening to their presentations, and sure enough, it was as I had suspected. Most of the things they were doing were terrible, but I usually thought one thing they said or did was good. I added these good things to my log and then studied it, memorized it, and used it with every prospect. By August of the second year, I had become the top salesperson in the new-car department. The manager said I could order my new Corvette. What I did not realize at the time was that it took about four months to get a Corvette. By the time my Corvette arrived at the dealership, it was December, and there was snow on the ground. We lived in upstate New York. If you know anything about Corvettes, you know that there is no way you can drive them in the snow. I was forced to settle for a Chevy Caprice with every option available. I loved it, and since we only had one car, I never could have used a Corvette anyway because we could not all fit in it.

However, the fact remained that I was the top salesperson in the dealership. Even though I used the Corvette as my motivation, I was still very proud of what I had done.

The next phase of my sales career came when I was introduced to a man who owned the largest heating-and-cooling company in our area. He loved to buy new trucks and had a large fleet of over sixty of them. Not long after meeting him, my good friend at the dealership told me that the owner of the heating company was interested in me for the position of sales manager at his company. He had twelve salespeople. I said I was interested and set up a meeting with him to talk about the job. He offered me a lot more money than I was making at the dealership, so I took the job. I was a great sales manager. I loved it there, and stayed for twenty-six years. I retired in June of 2004 with the company at record sales and earnings. My career at that company began with ten years as sales manager, then twelve years as a salesperson (I made a lot more money selling), and then finally seven years as sales manager again.

I spent ten years at the car dealership, twenty-six years at the heating company, and eleven years at my own consulting business, so I was in sales for a total of forty-seven years. I had many great experiences and made a lot of money. Wanting a new car and becoming a salesperson to get it were the best moves I ever made.

The only thing I miss since retiring is the training I did as a manager. I loved it, and I was good at it. I am so proud of all the people I turned into great salespeople, including my own sons, Michael & Robert. I learned so much because I remained a student of sales. Therefore, I decided to write this book and include the things in it that took me forty-seven years to learn. Now you do not have to wait forty-seven years to learn it.

It is all in this book for you to learn quickly and easily.

CHAPTER 1

So you want to be a Salesperson

Introduction to Sales

This book includes everything you need to know to be a salesperson. Not only does it include everything you need to decide if you should be a salesperson but also if you should go ahead and become a salesperson. I have included everything you need to learn in order to be successful at it. I have read many sales books, and I do not believe a book like this has ever been printed before. It is truly all-inclusive. I know you will enjoy it.

Welcome to the world of sales and I really mean welcome. You are about to enter a whole new world that is so exciting and so fulfilling that you will wonder why you didn't do this a long time ago.

Whether you are a brand-new salesperson or are already in sales, I guarantee you will enjoy reading this book. As you read on, you will see that this is not your typical sales book. I have been in sales for almost fifty years, and I still find it rewarding and exciting. No matter what happens, you will be glad you read this book, even if you never go into sales at all. I say that because you will find great ideas for having a happy life and positive motivation, setting goals, and ways to reach them.

This book will make you a better person no matter what your situation.

If you do go into or stay in the sales business, this book will make you the best salesperson you can be. If you read the whole book and do everything it says, you will be very successful, make many great friends, and have a better life. You will also earn large sums of money for you and your family. These are the reasons you bought this book in the first place.

If you read the preface, you know that I started out with no training or sales skills at all. I had a lot of confidence and motivation, but I soon realized that I would need a lot more skills to survive in the sales business.

If you want to be the best at this business, you will need to learn from your experiences.

This book will not get into things such as if the prospect is in their parent mode or in their child mode, if they are in left or right brain, or if they are a controller or passive or aggressive—none of that stuff. Throughout my career, I have never found this type of stuff very useful. I am not knocking it but rather just telling you about my experience with it. Remember, there is no such thing as bad sales training. You can learn from any training, even if you only learn that an approach just does not work.

I have designed this book for new salespeople who are just starting out. However, if you are an experienced salesperson, don't take this book back to the store; read it all the way through anyway. You will be a better person for it.

If you are just starting out or are thinking about being a salesperson, this chapter is especially for you.

I believe that sales are the best jobs in the whole world. If you are trying to decide if sales are what you want to do, you should be asking yourself the questions in the following sections.

The Qualities of a Good Salesperson

I believe all of the very best salespeople (including myself) have one quality in common: They get excited over every sale as if they just won the lottery. Many times the commission or bonus they get never enters their minds. All they want at the time is to get the sale. It's like a drug; it gets you high. It is like scoring the winning touchdown, hitting a big home run, or sinking that big putt. If you are a salesperson who gets this charge out of making the sale, then you are in the right profession. If, however, you do not get that charge out of getting the order, then I believe you might want to make a career change. I say that because while there are probably thousands of mediocre salespeople out there making a living, you will never be truly successful if you do not get that thrill out of closing the sale. Salespeople that have this quality can be spotted a mile away. When they make that big sale, they are as happy as they can be. All they can think about is what a great job they did. When they get back to the office, they tell anyone who will listen to them about the great job they did getting this order. If you see them in the hall or bathroom, they act as if they just won the lottery. I honestly do not know if this kind of excitement can be learned or if you have to be born with it. When you hear someone say, "He or she is a born salesperson," you can be sure that person has this quality.

Another quality that good salespeople have in common is recognizing that they do not know everything about sales. They constantly try to learn more and gain more knowledge about sales. Don't get me wrong; they will never show that they do not know everything about sales. If you talk to them, they will tell you that they know everything there is to know. However, inside they will always try to get better.

These top sellers also get excited when the company announces a sales-training course or seminar. When I hear salespeople react to this news as if someone just died, I get very concerned about their future. They obviously have no interest in furthering their sales career.

A great personality and social skills are also qualities of great salespeople. Do you know someone who always talks to people in an elevator or on a plane? These people make great salespeople because they love meeting and talking to people and enjoy finding out about them.

Successful salespeople dress for success and groom themselves to a T. They know that the first impression is the most important. While many salespeople do OK, they will never be top performers without this quality.

What Is Good About Being a Salesperson?

Most sales jobs give you a large amount of personal freedom. With this privilege comes a large amount of personal responsibility. You must be an independent self-starter because most of the time you will be unsupervised and on your own. This is particularly true if you will be doing outside sales. This unsupervised time must be spent meeting with prospects and existing clients and looking for new business. You absolutely cannot waste this time. You will end up making plenty of time for fun and family, but your working time must be spent on work. Hard, but rewarding work.

Perhaps the best thing about being a commissioned salesperson is the fact that your income potential is unlimited. Want a raise? Sell more. Your pay will generally not be left to your boss or supervisor to determine. How much money you make will be up to you. A high achiever is worth higher pay.

Another great benefit is the many new people you will meet all the time. If you are a very social person (and in sales, you better be), you are going to meet a lot of interesting people that you can learn a lot from even if you don't sell them anything. I am talking about life here, not sales.

Next, you do not spend all your time behind a desk. You get outside in the fresh air, in the cold, in the wind, in the rain. It is great; you will love it.

So many types of sales jobs exist that if you like to travel out of town a lot, you can find those kinds of jobs. These jobs usually involve overnight hotel stays. You should keep this in mind if you have a family. If you only want to drive around within an area that will get you home at night, plenty of jobs will allow you to do this. You may want to work as an inside salesperson, selling cars, furniture, appliances, home entertainment, and many other items. This would generally not involve travel at all.

While sales requires long hours and hard work, outside salespeople usually can set their time off, as they need it. While you are still busting your butt, you are the one to decide when you will be doing it. This may be a little harder to do if you have set hours as an inside salesperson. Also, keep in mind that the type of sales you go into will determine whether you will have to work nights or not.

There are two types of sales careers: wholesale and retail. Wholesale is selling to businesses, and retail is selling to the end user. In wholesale, you will be dealing with business owners, purchasing agents, and corporate officers. They usually require some type of entertainment (dinner, golf, lunch-type things), and this may mean some night appointments. However, since businesses are not open for salespeople at night in general, you will most likely not have to do night appointments.

Retail or selling to the end user will most likely result in working at night as most people work during the day and will only be able to see you at night. I always had to work at night but had time off during the day to get things done around the house or just relax. You will absolutely have to make time for fun and relaxation, alone or with your family, in order to be your very best when you are working and to rejuvenate yourself.

What Are the Drawbacks and How Do I Handle Them?

Overnight Travel

Overnight travel is the family killer for certain types of sales jobs. Make sure your family is OK with overnight travel if you choose this type of career. If you choose this type of sales, you must make time to spend with your spouse and family in order to be truly happy.

Many times in my sales career, I had to call upon my wife's understanding when I was unable to make it home for dinner, and in many cases, this was after I had told her that I would be home for dinner.

The Sales Slump

The sales slump happens to all of us at some time during our career. The pressure good salespeople put on themselves are sometimes unbearable. You must learn to handle this with the help of your spouse, significant other, or close friends. The worst thing about a sales slump is that you begin to question everything about yourself, your presentation, your job, and everything else in your life; you blame everything on your lack of sales. If you have been successful in the past, you should just keep on doing the things that made you successful. The worst thing you can do is change everything that made you great in the first place. The sales slump is a catch twenty-two; the more you need the sale, the worse you are at getting it. You will start exerting undue pressure on your prospects—and believe me, they will know it. So, just, relax, keep trying to get new prospects, and do what you do best.

Here are steps you should take to get out of a sales slump:

1. Find more people to talk to about your product.
2. Ask your manager for help and suggestions. (With some managers, this will do nothing to get more sales as they do not have a clue how to sell.) This will at least give the managers a good feeling about you because they will see that you recognize that you are not doing well and are willing to do something about it.

3. Try several new approaches that you have always wanted to do but were afraid you might lose customers because of it. In a sales slump, you have nothing to lose.

Fear of rejection can sometimes be a big problem in a sales career. Nobody likes being rejected. Remember when you met a girl or a guy that you liked and he or she told you to get lost? Not a good feeling. Well, in the sales business the number of times you are rejected vs. the number of prospects you talked to is known as your "closing average". In this case, the close means you got an order from that prospect. For example, if in a week you talked to twenty prospects and ended up selling something to ten of them, you would have a closing average for that week of 50 percent. Some products that you will sell will require a very small closing average in order to be very successful. I met a man at a seminar who was making over $300,000.00 a year selling farm equipment, and he had only a 10 percent closing average, which is considered very good in his business. For most salespeople, this is a terrible closing average. For most sales jobs, 50 percent is OK; 65 percent is good; and 75 percent is great. While he was doing great at 10 percent, he had a real problem with rejection because nine out of every ten prospects he talked to said no. As with any feeling of rejection, you must keep in mind that the prospects are not rejecting you personally, but rather the product or service you are selling. The prospects cannot reject you personally because they do not even know you. Always remember that. Here is another way to look at it. Let's say if you sell the product, you will earn $400.00 commission/bonus or extra above salary, or whatever way you are paid. Let's say you have a 33.3 percent closing average (that means if you sold to one out of three prospects you talked to, you get $400.00). Therefore, you talked to three people and made one sale with a commission of $400.00. In effect, you earned $133.33 for every person you talked to. If you look at it this way then the fear of rejection will not be so bad. (Each time you were rejected you made $133.33)

The best thing about closing average is that no matter what it is—10 percent or 75 percent—barring outside interference, such as bad economy, personal hardship, and things of that nature, it usually will not go down. By that, I mean that it is what it is for you. There is no reason for it to change unless you change. That means if you have a lousy closing average, you can still make a good living if you talk to a lot more people. No matter what your closing average is, the more people you talk to the more sales you will make. Simply put, if you have a 20 percent closing average, if you can talk to 100 prospects you will sell twenty of them. However, if you had a 60 percent closing average and talked to the same 100 prospects you would sell 60 of them. Therefore, you would make **three times more money** and spend the same amount of your selling time talking to the same 100 prospects. With more sales training and skill development, you can either work a lot less and make more sales and money or work sixteen hours a day and get rich. At any rate, you owe it to yourself to increase your closing average in order to be the best you can be. Once you have done this, you will be the one to decide how hard you want to work and how much money you want to make. Another big consideration will be if your boss is not happy with your closing average, you could be in big trouble. Look at it this way, if you owned a company that spent $50,000.00 dollars a month on advertising (such as TV, radio, newsprint and referrals) and brought in twenty leads on this day. Would you prefer to give them to salespeople with a 30 percent closing average or salespeople with a 65 percent closing average? The salespeople with the 30 percent would bring in six sales from twenty leads, but the salespeople with the 65 percent would bring in thirteen sales from the same twenty leads. If I owned this company, I would not want many 30 percent closing average people on my sales force.

You're Emotions

I do not think that—with the exception of professional sports—there is another career in the world that sends you to the heights of pleasure and excitement and then plunges you to despair in such a short period. You must learn to handle these swings and not let them bother you (see chapter 2: Your Motivation).

What Can I Expect?

If this is your first trip down the sales road, you will need to know what to expect. By that, I mean that you will have many questions about this great career. I will try to answer the questions you might have in this section.

How many hours a week will I have to work?

Of course, this will depend on the type of sales job you select. In general, you will most likely have to put in about sixty to seventy hours a week. This may seem like a lot, but I think you will enjoy it. You will also find it very rewarding. If you are an outside salesperson, you will be moving around a lot and will never be bored. In many cases, the hours you put in will be your choice. You may be able to set your own schedule and plan time off when it will work into your schedule.

What will my manager do for me?

This has always been a sore subject for me because I never had the luxury of a good manager. My idea of a good manager is one who takes full responsibility for his or her salespeople, and if they are doing poorly, the manager must find out what the problem is and work hard to correct it. I believe that if a salesperson fails, the manager has also failed. This is especially true if the manager was the one who hired the salesperson. I always felt I was a good sales manager, but I did fail in some instances to make good salespeople out of the people I hired. I felt bad about this; nevertheless, I accepted it as my fault, not theirs.

A good manager must know how to motivate the sales force to help the salespeople get the job done, and a good manager must see that the sales department always reaches its preset sales and profit goals no matter what. This is why the company has a sales manager in the first place. When I started out as a sales manager, our sales department was not reaching its goals. The owner of the company called me into his office and told me we were way behind in reaching our goals. I just sat there and did not say anything until finally I agreed with him, as I knew this was true. He said something to me that I later realized was the true essence of the sales manager's job. He asked me what I was doing about it. This struck me like a ton of bricks. He was absolutely right. It was my responsibility to take action and make things happen, not his. He gave me all the tools I needed to get the job done. All I had to do was to come up with new ideas for training and marketing to do what needed to be done.

The bottom line is that you may be lucky and get a manager who will help you in every way to be successful. However, if you get a manager who is not qualified or who got the job because he or she married the boss's daughter or son, it does not mean you are all washed up. You can work with these people, but just don't ask for help because you will not get it. The simple answer is that all you need to learn is to motivate yourself (see chapter 2: Your Motivation).

How Much Money Can I Make?

The average salesperson in this country makes between $50,000.00 and $100,000.00 per year. In addition, some get company cars and other spiffs, such as bonuses or contest rewards and free trips. Top performers can make a lot more. I know salespeople making over $1,000,000.00 a year. If you have to pay for your own car and other expenses, it does not mean that this is not a good job. If you are making a lot of money, it is not a problem. In addition, your expenses for work-related items (at least at the time of this writing) are tax deductible if you are not reimbursed for them.

What Will My Life Be Like?

You will have a great life. There is one very important thing that will make your life great: You must enjoy selling as a career. If you do not enjoy it, get out now. No one should spend their life working at a job they do not like. It is not worth it. An old quote that was told to me when I started in my sales career is "Do a job that you love to do and you will never work a day in your life". Remember, the goal in life is to be happy.

I made a list for my salespeople of all the things I wanted in a career and asked them to do the same. I encourage you to do the same.

My list looked like this:

a. I do not want to sit behind a desk all day.
b. I like to drive.
c. I do not want to be out of town overnight.
d. I want to have flexible hours.
e. I want to be outside part of the time, but I do not want to be out a lot when it is too cold or too hot.
f. I want to work where there is a good support team.
g. I want a feeling of accomplishment.
h. I do not want my boss hanging over me all the time.

i. I want to be able to take some company trips.
j. I want to be rewarded for a job well done.
k. I want to be recognized for my efforts.
l. I want to earn a good pay.
m. I want to meet interesting people.
n. I want to be proud of what I do.
o. When I retire, I want to be able to say I helped many people.

Do this for yourself and go look for a career that meets as many if not all the thing you put on your list.

What Will My Boss Expect of Me?

In most sales jobs, you will be given a quota or goal that will be tailored just for you. When you are new, your goal will most likely be lower. As you grow and get more familiar with the product or service you are selling, your goal will be raised. You will be expected to reach these goals. If you do not, you may be given extra training or your manager may spend more time with you. If you are not motivated or are not trying to be better, you most likely will be fired.

You will be expected to be on time for meetings, and you will need to fill out many forms and do a lot of paperwork. You will be expected to manage your time to be very efficient. You will need to learn computer skills and use an iPod or similar device to help you manage all the other things you are expected to do. Your company will expect you to have a positive attitude and be open to change (see chapter 2: Your Motivation).

Will I Have To Relocate?

This depends on the company. If you choose a large company with many offices around your state or all over the country, you will most likely be offered relocation at some time with your company. On the other hand, if you select a company that only has one location in the area you want to live in, you will not be asked to relocate. If the time comes that you are asked to relocate, you may have to go or lose your job. In some cases, the choice will be up to you whether to move or not. You should be aware, however, that if you turn down a transfer too many times, your position in the company might not be the same as it was. By this, I mean that you may be passed over for a promotion or that your opinion in many matters will not be asked for any more. The good part about relocating is that it usually involves a promotion or increase in pay. In addition, if your company has many offices, you may have the opportunity to transfer if you want to.

Do I Need a College Degree?

This has always been an absolute must for me. I never went to college, and during my life, I had many doors slammed in my face because I did not have a college degree. Some sales jobs do not require a degree; however, as you progress within almost any job you may not have the opportunity to advance without a degree. When a company or any employer considers you for a promotion, the first thing they will want to know is "what is your degree in?" As soon as you say you do not have one, the employer will say, "Thank you very much, but we need someone with a degree for this position." In many cases, the employer does not even care what your degree is in, only the fact that you have one. This not only applies to a sales job but to just about any job where ever you are employed. At a local Cadillac dealer where I live, you need a degree to sell cars. The bottom line is if you have a degree, you are in good shape for anything you want to try. If you do not, at least you know what to expect, and you might want to consider going back to get a degree or attending night school or getting your degree on line. At some time during your career, you will wish you had one.

What Is the One Thing I Will Need?

The absolute number one thing you will need is a *positive attitude*. There are only two times you will need a good attitude. When you are asleep and when you are awake. You must keep trying to get it and keep it your whole life. At your job no matter what your career or type of work, if you get the title of "having a bad attitude" trust me on this, you will be fired. You will be the bad apple in the bunch. You will be the person who is dragging everyone else down. Do not let this happen to you. (More to follow on this)

What If I Am Not the Most Beautiful Person Around?

I will not lie to you about being attractive. The better looking you are, the more chances you will get to make a sale. All other things being equal, people buy from people they like and trust not whether they are attractive or not. Initially, however they like to talk to attractive people more. The good news is that you can make up for this by having a great personality and being honest with prospects. They need to get to know you better and be impressed with your sincerity, empathy, and honesty. They will buy from someone they like and trust.

If you keep yourself neat and clean and if you let the prospect get to know you, the fact that you are not attractive will have no or very little effect on how much you sell.

What Kind of Pay Plans Are There?

Unlike most jobs, which are salary or hourly, weekly, or biweekly pay, sales jobs pay plans generally include some type of commission for the products or services you sell. Below is a list of the different types of sales plans you may run into.

1. **Straight commission:** In this plan, a salesperson is paid a fee for each product or service he or she sells in a given month. For example, if you get a $25.00 commission for every service agreement you sell and you sold two hundred service agreements this month, then at the end of the month, you would get a $5,000.00 commission. I always said that if the company sets the commission right on a product or service that will maintain its required margin (profit), then it would never have an overpaid salesperson. The salespeople are paid exactly what they are worth. If the salespeople sell a lot, then they will be paid a lot. If they sell a little, they will be paid a little—at least until the time comes when they are fired.

   This used to be the most popular type of pay plan for salespeople, and I really like this plan a lot because the company or your manager has no say in how much money you make. You control your pay. Over the years, it became much harder for companies to hire good salespeople on this type of plan because employees wanted a steady paycheck, and they never knew how much money they were going to make in advance. In particular, sometimes sales could be slow due to problems at the supplier that could cause shortages of the product or if the product or service was seasonal. Maybe the salesperson was just having a bad month. In these cases, many salespeople did not have enough money to pay mortgages or car payments that were due on a monthly basis. Therefore, some companies decided to add a new twist to the straight commission plan, called draw-against commission.

2. **Draw-against commission:** In this plan, the company pays you a set or sometimes a variable amount each week, the total of which will be deducted from your monthly commission. Using the example above, you have earned a total of $5,000.00 for the month. The company has advanced you, say, $800.00 per week for four weeks (some months

have five weeks). Therefore, it already gave you $3,200.00 of the $5,000.00 it owes you. In this case, you would get a $1,800.00 commission check at the end of the month. This is a good plan if you are worried about being able to pay bills that come up before you get your final month's check. Keep in mind, however, that if in this example you only sold one hundred service agreements for the month, you would have commissions totaling $2,500.00 for the month. However, the company already paid you $3,200.00. This means that you owe the company $700.00 at the end of that month. In most cases, this is OK as long as you make enough commissions the next month to make up the difference. This means that if next month you earn $4,000.00 in commissions and the company advanced you $800.00 per week for four weeks, your draw for that month is $3,200.00, but you owe them $700.00 from the previous month. Now the company adds $700.00 to this month's draw of $3,200.00; you now owe them $3,900.00. You earned $4,000.00, so your commission check for this month is $100.00.

The one thing to keep in mind with this plan is that if you keep having a negative at the end of each month, the company will most likely have a limit that you can owe them. If you exceed that limit, your draw may be cut off until the balance is paid back in full, or you may end up being fired. If the company fires you, generally you do not have to pay back the amount you owe them.

3. **Salary + Commission:** In this plan, you get a salary each week that does not have to be paid back. In addition, you will get a reduced commission for each product or service you sell for that month.

4. **Salary + Commission + Bonus:** A bonus can be used with any of the pay plans listed and may work like this: Let's say you sold two hundred service agreements at $25.00 per

agreement and earned $5,000.00. The company has figured out that if you sell 150 for the month, it will reach its sales goals and required margin (profit). Therefore, it would decide to pay you a bonus of $15.00 for every service agreement over 150 that you sell. That means you would be paid $25.00 each for the first 150 or $3,750.00 plus $40.00 each for the next fifty or $2,000.00. Therefore, your commission for this month would be a total of $5,750.00 instead of the $5,000.00 in the first example. You would end up with a $750.00 bonus for the month.

The most important thing to keep in mind about your pay is that the company is going to pay what you are worth no matter what pay plan it may have. If, for example, the company has figured out that your sales each year (barring any misfortune) should bring you a pay of $60,000.00 and a company profit of say 15 percent. It has determined that with you making that amount it will reach its sales goals and end up with the required margin (profit), and then you can call the pay anything you want: salary, commission, draw, or bonus. The bottom line is that if you meet your goals, then the company can afford to pay you $60,000.00. From its standpoint, commissions are better because it does not have to pay you up front. In either case, however, if you continue *not* making the company's goals, you will most likely be fired.

Many companies use non-monetary incentives to motivate their salespeople to excel. These may include:

1. Trips
2. Prizes
3. Special recognition (i.e., the salesperson of the month might get special privileges, expense

accounts, membership in top sales clubs, or anything that will motivate the sales force to be the best
they can be)

In my many years of sales management, I have found that if you
ask any salesperson, "What motivates you to sell more?" he or she
will always answer, "Cash." However, in every case I have found this
not to be true. I could always get salespeople to do more with trips
and prizes than with cash. You could give a salesperson $1,000.00
in cash for going all out during a sales contest, but he or she will
work much harder for a trip that only cost the company $700.00. I
always got more bang for the buck with a trip. It was always a win-
win situation for the company and for the salesperson.

CHAPTER 2

Your Motivation

Throughout the rest of this book, look for "Try
it, it works" at the end of a subject.
Do these things and you will be amazed by how well they work.

Why Should I be Motivated?

In sales as in life, you will be far better off with a positive attitude and happy motivation. Some things in life are not happy situations, as you all know, but having a positive attitude does not mean that you can't be sad or melancholy or that you have to be happy with everything someone says or does to you. It does mean that you do not stay sad or melancholy very long. It means that you can disagree with someone and look for a solution to a disagreement that will be beneficial to all parties, that you can look hard for good in all situations, and that you can find the good in something and not go looking for all the bad in every situation.

Why do we always look for the bad? You do not have to look for the bad because it comes to you all the time without you looking for it. In Zig Zigler's book *Born to Win* (which I think is a necessary book to read for everyone), he sums up best why you should be a "good finder." He says, "When you dig for gold, you have to move a lot of dirt, but you are not looking for dirt, you are looking for gold." Yes, you will see a lot of dirt; you will get it on you and in your face, and you will be surrounded by it. Always remember to get rid of the dirt if you want to find the gold. Think back to a recent situation in which someone or something made a change in your life. Maybe it was your son or daughter starting school or college, or maybe your boss asked you to move offices or announced changes in the company. I will bet the first thing that went through your mind was "What is bad about this?" Be honest: When your son started college, you wondered, "How am I going to pay for this?" If your boss asked you to change offices, you thought, "That office is cold and damp and is far away from the main office." Instead of these thoughts, you could have thought, "***Wow***, my son is starting college. I am so proud of him. He is a great kid and will be great at whatever he chooses. Now my wife and I can spend some quality time together at last." Similarly, you could think that the new office has a great view, and maybe you will like being farther away from the main office because they will not be bothering you all the time. You see, the good part about having a positive attitude is that ***it makes you feel better than a negative attitude.*** It is all summed up for you right here and that is the bottom line. Why would you not want to feel better? I believe the answer to the age-old question of "what is the meaning of life" is "to be happy."

I further believe that in order to be truly happy, you will need to be honest, law abiding, generous, empathetic, faithful, understanding, and helpful. You should also believe in a higher power, limit your consumption of alcohol, avoid inappropriate language, magazines, and videos, and take care of your health and the health of your family and friends. Some people think that having money makes you happy. Come on now; you know that is not true. You know people with money or fame that are truly unhappy. No, you must have all of the above in order to be truly happy. If you leave one of them out, then it will lead to situations that can make you the unhappiest person in the world. You must have them all.

Having a positive attitude will help you cope with the bad as it comes along. It will not eliminate it, but it will let you deal with it and move on.

Many times people have said to me that their boss said they should have a positive attitude. However, what the boss really meant was *they* should agree with him or her all the time. This is true; many people want **you** to have a positive attitude, but they think they do not need one. For many bosses, it means that you do everything they tell you or else you have a bad attitude. Well, you need to have a good attitude for you, not for your company. You can have a good attitude at work and still not agree with everything that they do to you; just be sure you look for the good in it. The bad parts will not seem as bad, and if it's really bad, it will probably be changed in the near future or that boss will be fired, change jobs, or something. If you find that you really cannot put up with it, do not walk around telling everyone what a lousy decision it was. Instead, confront the boss with the problem about what he said or did with positive comments. If it means that much to you in the end, solve the problem with two words: *I quit.*

In conclusion, the answer to the question "Why should I be motivated?" is that motivation makes you feel good about yourself and better able to handle adversity.

How Do I get Motivated?

First, you need to avoid all the de-motivators listed in the previous paragraph. In order to help you be successful, you should avoid negative people at all costs. These people always talk about all the bad at work, or they talk about people who are sick or dying or maybe how bad they always feel. While you might have to talk about these things on occasion, you should not dwell on these subjects very long. Always remember the difference between empathy and sympathy. Sympathy means you understand how someone feels, and empathy is feeling as someone feels. Avoid the latter whenever possible.

Read good motivational books. This type of reading will serve to lift you up and reinforce your happy motivation.

Do not worry about things you cannot change. If you really cannot do anything about a situation, then do not spend your time worrying about it. I know this is easier said than done, but if you work hard at it, you can learn how to do it *and* keep your mind working on positive things.

Get yourself deep in debt. *I am just kidding.* However, if you buy something that really means a lot to you, you will be motivated to get the money you need to be able to pay for it.

Have a desire for the better things in life. I have seen some salespeople that just did not want anything; they were happy making low pay and never desired the best in life. I found out that most of these people had never been exposed to the best that life has to offer, so if you are like this, go out and rent a Corvette, take a trip to Europe and stay in the finest hotels, or rent a sixty-foot yacht. See how you like these things. Some people like these sorts of things, but others are just as happy without them. If this does not motivate you to do better than you are now doing, congratulations, you have fulfilled the meaning of life: *to be happy.* However, since your boss may not be happy with the same level of pay and sales as you, you may be in for some bad news very soon. Always try to keep a positive attitude.

A long time ago, I used to get so upset with other drivers on the road and was infuriated when someone cut me off or changed lanes right in front of me. If someone was driving too slowly in front of me, I had a fit and cursed at them. When a red light was too long, I wanted to call the highway department and ream them out for this long light. After I decided to get a positive attitude, I realized this was stupid. The person that cut me off went on their merry way and was not bothered at all, while it ruined my whole day. In most instances, the person at fault just made a mistake. We all make mistakes while driving, and some people pay a very dear price for their mistake. Let it go at that.

Get Yourself A Good Self-Image.

A warning sign of a poor self-image is constant bragging. These people need to constantly build themselves up to keep reminding themselves that they are the best. People with good self-image do not need to do this because they have a quiet inner peace, and they know that they are great. People with good self-image spend time trying to build others up, and they get satisfaction from this. People with poor self-mage give too much emphasis to material things. They think that the more and better material things they have will prove how successful they are. The strange thing is that this does not improve their self-image, and they need to keep getting more stuff to keep telling themselves they are better than everyone else is. They always talk about themselves, and in conversations with other people, they must always butt in and change the topic to talk about themselves and how good they are. You will notice that they always tell you what you should do and say *I have this and you should get one as I did*. On any subject, they will say *you should do this or that as I did*, and they will rarely ask you to tell them about something you have done. If they do, it's only to set you up for their next "you should" lecture.

People with poor self-image

a. They do not take criticism well. Most of us do not, but they take it much harder and fight back with everything they have. They will always point a finger at someone else to take the blame for their failures.
b. They are uncomfortable when alone. When these people are alone, they are unable to build themselves up.
c. They like to spread negative gossip because they want to be the first person to tell you the bad news. They are extremely disappointed when they find out you heard something before they did.

The way to a good self-image is to avoid the above-listed traits and to keep your mind and body healthy. You are striving for inner confidence, and you cannot get it by drinking, cheating, lying, stealing, swearing, looking at pornography, or doing anything else bad you can think of. If you have a bad self-image, avoid all of the above, and I guaranty you will be amazed at how much better you feel. You will develop a great self-image and exude confidence.

You might ask why you need a good self-image and why you should exude confidence to be a good salesperson. The answer is **you don't.** You may know great salespeople who do not have a good self-image as evidenced by behaviors listed above. However, I will guarantee you that they do not get as much pleasure and fun from their sales as they could with a good self-image. It certainly helps; remember that people buy from people they like and trust. Your confidence tells them you are a professional and will treat them right. If you avoid traits from the bad self-image list, they will like you. One of the best salespeople I know has no selling skills at all. He sells by showing prospects confidence that what he is going to do for you is exactly what you need. No one else on earth can provide the same product and service he can. If you believe this, you have to buy from him. Whenever you eliminate a habit that is self-destructive in your mind, you build your self-image. *Try it; it works.*

Get Some Enthusiasm.

I learned this from a prospect I met once early in my sales career. As I went through my presentation, I noticed that the customer was getting very excited about everything I said. The strange thing was that the more excited he got, the more excited I got. By the time I had closed the sale, I was more excited about the benefits my product was going to provide this customer than I had ever been. As I left his home with the order, I asked myself what was wrong with this picture. The customer had gotten me excited; I should have been the one to get him excited. Later, I tried this, and many times my customers got so excited over the product, they just bought it without chiseling down the price or making any other objections. What a great sales tool.

Try it; it works.

How Do I Avoid Being De-Motivated?

Be around positive people. Do not let bad things get you down. Always look for the good in any situation. If your boss chews you out, do not take it personally. Remember that it is only business, not your life. When your wife, husband, boyfriend, girlfriend, kids, boss, or anyone else turns you down, start the sales process of trying to change his or her mind. If this does not work, do not let it bother you. You will get over it soon.

Throughout your sales career, you will attend meetings where the boss has singled you out for criticism. You must not let this bother you. A good manager would never do this. His or her criticism of you should be in private, such as in an office. However, as I mentioned earlier, you most likely will not have a good manager. They are very rare indeed, so accept their mistake and realize that they most likely have a reason for telling you this. While you may be mad that they did it in public, you should still try to correct the problem they were referring to. Do not let it ruin your day by complaining to everyone you see. Just forget how he or she did it and correct it. One thing I always asked myself when this happened to me was "Will I remember this a year from now?" If the answer was no, I blew it off and forgot it.

Try it; it works.

Do not let other people tear you down. These people have no interest in seeing you succeed. Avoid them at all costs. People who love you or care about you will not bring you down. Surround yourself with their support.

Try it; it works.

Do not get involved in bitch sessions with your peers. It will not help you at all, and it is a waste of time. If you have a problem with something, go tell someone who can correct the problem. Complaining to your peers will only get you a reputation for having a bad attitude and resisting change. I met the owner of a very large business in California at a seminar, and he told me that the only way you could be fired at his company was to have a bad attitude. *No other reason.* He was a multimillionaire. The top salesperson in many companies will eventually be fired if they have a bad attitude and fight change. The company cannot afford these types of people. They bring everyone down and spread their resistance to change all over the company. A good company must change as time goes by in order to be more productive or more competitive. If you have to learn just one thing in your sales career and in life, it should be to embrace change. Things change; get used to it, and learn to use it to your advantage.

Three things about change that you need to learn:

1. Things will change.
2. Learn to make the best of it.
3. If you cannot live with it, get out. Do not spend your life being miserable about it.

CHAPTER 3

Setting Goals

Why do I need goals? The answer is so that you know how you are doing. Imagine playing a soccer game with no goals; everyone would run up and down the field kicking the ball around. After about an hour of this, someone would ask, "How are we doing?" Everyone would look at each other and say, "I don't know, but I think we are doing well." I think so too. Are we ahead of the other team? Well, no one knows who is ahead or who won the game. We just do not know.

You see, you need goals to show your progress. This is true for everyone, not just salespeople. Goals need to be a part of your life. Some things you may want to set goals for are:

a. A new home
b. A new car
c. College (for yourself or your kids)
d. Retirement
e. Relationships
f. Losing weight
g. Stop smoking
h. Get healthy
i. Financial independence

j. Sports
k. Self-image
l. Positive attitude
m. Motivation
n. A place at the lake
o. Lower stress
p. Being a better husband, wife, father, mother, uncle, aunt
q. Your career

I think you get the idea. You will need two types of goals: short-term (these will lead up to the second) and long-term goals. Let's say, as an example, that a long-term goal of yours is financial independence. Here is an example of what your goal outline might look like:

1. <u>Clearly define the exact goal</u>
   I want to have enough money so that I can do what I want to do and not have to work at a job.
2. <u>Set a specific date to reach the goal</u>
   Twenty-five years from now
3. <u>How much net worth will I need to reach this goal?</u>
   Two million dollars
4. <u>List problems you will need to overcome</u>
   a. I am not a good salesperson now, but I will learn more selling skills.
   b. I need to get a better job. I will put out resumes to companies that provide good pay and unlimited potential.
   c. I am not a good money manager. I will take courses for financial planning, and I will hire a firm to invest most of my savings for the goal.
   d. I have nothing now.

<u>Identify companies, groups, and people that you can use to reach the goals</u>

My company's 401K.
My financial planner.
My father has had great success.
My uncle knows how to invest wisely.
My local college has some great courses I could take.

Now, I must make a list of the short-term goals that if reached will guarantee reaching the long-term goals. (This is the *how am I doing* part.)

I need $2 million in twenty-five years, which means that I need to break this down per year. The early years will not have my net worth growing as fast as the later years, so let's break the goal down into three-year segments and then again into one-year segments. By the end of three years, if I have $100,000.00, I should be in good shape. That means I need $34,000.00 a year for three years, and that means if I can triple that in the next three years, I will be on target. Then by the end of six years, I will have $300,000.00. Now, I have some serious money to invest, but between my 401K and other investments, I am only getting 5 percent return, so at this point I might buy some rental property or some property to fix up and sell to make a profit.

At the end of each year, you will do a net-worth study to determine if you are reaching your short-term goals. If you are not, all is not lost. You must rethink how you are obtaining wealth and what you can do to improve your return. Remember, the course to your long-term goal will not always be smooth. Many things can happen along the way that may set you back. For example, your kids may need braces, and it is going to cost $10,000.00 to fix them. You redo your entire plan to include this cost as a negative in reaching your goal, but you must never lower the goal.

A plane takes off from New York City for a landing in Los Angeles, but when the plane is over Nevada, the air-traffic controllers tell the pilot that there is a very dangerous storm on their course about one hundred miles ahead. The co-pilot tells the passengers about the bad storm; and that the captain has decided to go back to New York and try again tomorrow when the weather is better. Yeah, right, this would never happen. When the plane took off from New York, the pilot's goal was to land in Los Angeles, and he was not going to change his goal because of bad weather ahead. Instead, he plans a new course that will allow him to go above or around the storm and still land in Los Angeles. He may have to speed up a little in order to reach his goal on time, but he will not change the goal.

I think you can see how we will proceed from here, so I will not continue for the next nineteen years. Always remember that you need to set short-term goals in order to reach the long-term goal.

Here are some suggestions for areas in which to set goals.

1. Career examples
   a. Get a better job
   b. Sell more stuff
   c. Become a manager
   d. Become vice president
   e. Get a master's degree
2. Financial examples
   a. Make more money
   b. Invest in real estate
   c. Save for early retirement

d. Get a second home
e. Get a classic car
3. Physical examples
   a. Lose weight
   b. Build more muscle
   c. Stop drinking
   d. Stop smoking
   e. Set an exercise program
   f. Have plastic surgery
4. Mental examples
   a. Have a positive attitude
   b. Be more motivated
   c. Be more understanding
   d. Show more affection
   e. Don't be a grouch
   f. Write a book
5. Social examples
   a. Be friendlier
   b. Be less shy
   c. Be a better listener
   d. Be on time
   e. Be a more courteous driver
   f. Be less boring
   g. Have more sympathy
   h. Be more generous
6. Spiritual examples
   a. Go to church or synagogue more often
   b. Participate in church or synagogue activities
   c. Pray more
   d. Read the Bible or literature about your religion

As you can see, there are small and big goals that we all have. We must first realize that they are goals and not just wishes. We can reach goals, but wishes rarely come true. The process for reaching goals is the same for each goal big or small. First, the long-term goal and then the short-term goals to judge how we are doing. Remember, if you just have the long-term goal, you will not find out how you are doing until it is too late to do anything about it.

Now, if you bought this book to learn how to sell, then hold on to your hat because the rest of this book will blow you away with everything you want to know.

In addition, remember:

Try it; it works.

CHAPTER 4

The Building Blocks to the Sale

The sale is made up of small building blocks. The more blocks you put in, the stronger the foundation will be and the closer you get to the sale. If, for example, you are a man and like to have a beard or if you are a woman and like to wear very short skirts, you will most likely offend only a very small portion of the public. Since the people who will not buy from you are a very small minority, it cannot hurt you. Right or wrong? Why would you do something that will lose any sales? You want all you can get. I do not know anyone that is offended by a clean-shaven man or a skirt just above the knee. So, one of the building blocks is to be clean-shaven and wear normal-length skirts. You do not have to do this, but be aware that these things are costing you sales. You may still be successful if you ignore small matters, but you are losing sales. Do not fool yourself into thinking otherwise.

Some people in this country still will not buy from people driving a foreign car, so if you choose to do this, know that it is costing you sales. Many of these building blocks are for in-home sales. Just remove any that do not apply to your type of sales.

Here is my list of building blocks for the sale.

a. Dress properly for the product you are selling (a suit and tie is not appropriate for selling to construction workers).
b. Be well groomed.
c. Be sympathetic. (You understand how someone feels.)
d. Be exactly on time for appointments (early means you are not on time, and late means you are wasting the prospect's time).
e. Don't talk politics or religion with the prospect. If he or she asks your opinion of a politician, just say, "He (or she) has a tough job. I am glad I don't have to do it."
f. Never drink alcoholic beverages with the prospect. Say, "Thank you, but I never drink while I am working." (Entertaining prospects would be an exception.)
g. Have all the information, brochures, and order forms you need to get the job done.
h. Smile a lot.
i. Be sincere.
j. Learn to listen.
k. Be understanding.
l. Be cheerful.
m. Don't brag about yourself (only as it relates to your qualifications).
n. Know your product or service.
o. Never use foul language.
p. Never argue with the prospect (win the argument; lose the sale).
q. Never interrupt the prospect.
r. Include all people present in your presentation.
s. Tell stories (as they relate to your product or service).

t. Don't take or make calls on your cell phone while with the prospect.
u. Give sincere compliments.
v. Laugh a lot.
w. Remove your shoes or put booties on (do not get the floor dirty).
x. Ask before you place your briefcase down somewhere.
y. If you have to survey the home, ask permission before opening cabinets or doors.
z. If you are a man, stand up when a woman enters or leaves the room.
    aa. Be friendly to the dog.
    bb. Be friendly to the kids.
    cc. Never act as if you are in a hurry.
    dd. ***Don't ask dumb questions, such as:***
        1. Are you going to buy today?
        2. Am I wasting my time here?
        3. Are you married?
        4. Are you divorced?
        5. Do you live alone?
        6. When will your husband or wife be home?
        7. Can I make a commission on you?
        8. Are you getting other bids?
        9. Will you buy if I give you a good price?
        10. Whose cigars are these?

I think you are getting the idea.

People may volunteer this information but you should **not** ask for it. You can find out this information by asking other related questions and things that you see or learn as you go through your presentation. Such as "Will there be anyone else involved in this decision other than yourself who might want to listen in"?

Ask questions that may get the prospect to brag about a son, daughter, wife, or husband or maybe a hobby or collection he or she has, such as:

1. Do you play golf?
2. Are your kids in college?
3. Do you play sports?
4. Do you collect stamps (if you see stamps around)?
5. Did you play football (if you see football trophies around)?
6. Are you an artist (if you see paintings around)?
7. Who does your lawn (if they have a beautiful lawn)?
8. Do you ski (if you see skis around)?

In order to be a good salesperson, you must first understand why people buy. Here is a brainteaser for you. Can you think of any product or service that was not sold to someone at one time or another? List them below. However, remember that it must have never been sold ever.

_____

_____

_____

CHAPTER 5

Selling to Women

Y ou might very well ask why a subject like this would appear in a book about sales in this age of political correctness. Well, I would not blame you for asking. The fact remains, however, that selling to a woman is different from selling to a man. Let's look at why. When I started selling in 1968, knowing how to sell to women was not a big deal because men made most household decisions. Today we have seen a big change in women's rolls. They now make or are consulted in almost all household decisions. In addition, there are many more woman head of households.

Women have come a long way from 1968 and I do not think they did it at the expense of men but rather in cooperation with men. The fact that I want to get across to you is that there is no longer a mold for women to fit in. If you are a woman, you know that better than I do. I will not say to you that I understand anything at all about women, and I do not think any man can. I will however, tell you what makes them buy.

If You Are a Man or a Woman Salesperson

The first thing you should know is that there are several different categories of women,

(As well as several different categories of men).

1. Some women still like having a man make all the decisions for them. Don't make the mistake of thinking they have all disappeared.
2. Some women like to share the decision making with their partner.
3. Some women either want or have to make all the decisions. (They have no one to help them)
4. Some women hate men. You need to be able to sell to them.

The first thing you need to find out is what category the female prospect you are about to talk to falls into. Let's take them one at a time. This is also true if you are a female salesperson.

The woman who wants the man to make all the decisions: In many cases, this woman has been asked by her male partner to collect all the information she can from several different companies so that he could look over all the proposals later and make the final decision as to which company they will buy from. This is true of most products, including:

a. A new car
b. A new refrigerator
c. A new heating or air-conditioning system
d. New fencing
e. New carpeting
f. Any new product that is considered an average expense

Do not however; make the mistake of thinking the woman will not make the final decision. In many cases, she will. Here is what typically happens: A salesperson comes to the home or the woman goes to the place of business. The woman picks up brochures on the product and gets prices and other information from a salesperson. She brings all of it home for her partner to review, and when he sees something he likes, he calls the salesperson and asks him to come out and show him what the salesperson already showed his wife or female partner so that they can go ahead and buy the product. Alternatively, in the case of sales that are made from a place of business or a showroom, the man goes there to make the final decision. As a male salesperson, you must figure out not only that this woman is not going to make the decision to go ahead but also the kind of relationship she has with her partner or husband.

Here is how it works: You show up at the home or the woman shows up at your place of business. You begin to talk to her by asking if you can help her. She might give you a clue at this time that she will not be making a decision on this product by saying that her husband or partner has sent her out to collect information about the product you sell. This is great because you now know she is not the decision maker in this instance. If she does not give you a clue, you still need to find out. You cannot just ask her, so you ask her questions such as:

a. Is this (your product) for yourself? (She may tip her hand at this point). She might say it is for her and her husband or her partner. You did it. You found out that she is either married or buying it with her boyfriend. *Or did you?* What if her partner turns out to be a woman? You would be in big trouble if you assumed wrong.

b. Are you familiar with this _____ (the product). She might say no, but my husband is.

c. Would you like to learn more about _____? If she says no, do not waste your time trying to explain it. If she says yes, give her a quick overview of how your product works and what it will do for them. She might say no, I am just getting information together.

At any rate, this is how you find out if she is living with a man, living alone, or living with a woman. You need to know this because if there is a man involved, you still need to find out if she needs him to help make the decision. All right, so you went through all this and determined that she lets the man make all the decisions, and she is just collecting information. The first thing you better learn is not to try to sell her anything, and even if you succeed, you will lose because her husband or partner will be furious with you for pressuring her into a sale—even if you didn't do it—and will cancel the order. Remember that she will be a salesperson for you when she gets home to her husband or partner. You need to have her remember the important parts about you and your company, and she must be impressed that out of all the salespeople she talked to that day, you were the most knowledgeable, the most courteous, and the most concerned about her need for information. You must treat her with respect, and do not suggest that she come back with her husband before you help her with what she is looking for because this suggests to her that you think she is too stupid to make this decision without her husband or any man. She must go home and tell her husband that you not only had the best product but also were the most helpful and courteous to her. Now, at some point you should get her to call her husband on the phone to find out more information for you if she is unable to answer a question you asked, such as which model would be best for them. Many times this is not possible, but in some cases, she will be able to get him on the phone so you can talk to him. I do not really care what you talk to him about as long as he remembers you and how nice you were to him and his wife. Now, when it comes time to narrow down the field as to who they will buy from, it may very well turn out that you were the only salesperson that got to talk to him. In most cases, you will be in the running for the sale. Remember that if you are an in-home salesperson, you handle everything the same way.

The women who likes to share the decision making process.

They may want to share the decision with _____: You fill in the blank.

Her husband, her partner, her father, her sister, the neighbor. It could be anyone. It does not mater who. You treat them all the same. You can use all the above means to find out what you need to know about who will make the final decision to go ahead and purchase your product. The only difference is that you must now be sure to give your presentation to all parties that will be decision makers. This is the most common method for most people.

The women who either wants or has to make all the decisions.

This woman in many cases has no one to help her make the buying decision. If you can find this out then you must make every effort to help her make the decision to buy from you. You will need to go out of your way to make sure she has all the information she needs in order to make a good decision. You will need to build a rapport with her so that she will like you and trust you.

The woman who hates men.

Yes, they are out there and if you are a salesperson, you will eventually meet one. Here is how you handle this. It will not take long to realize whom you are talking to. The first thing you will notice is that there are no man things in this home or business. No men's shoes, no after shave, no hot rod magazines, no footballs and so on. In this situation, you must be sure to keep everything generic. That is, you can in no way imply that she will need a man's help in anything that she might want or do. She will not need a plumber, she will not need an electrician, and she will not need a carpenter or any one that would imply that she would need a man for anything that needs to be done in her home or business. Aside from that you will need to treat her with all do respect and answer all her questions honestly and try to build some rapport with her. This will not be easy but you can do it. Please remember that if you are a man possibly other salespersons have been there and walked out because of the way she treated them. In addition, if you are a woman you may still have problems with her if you rely too much on talking about your husband or boy friend if you have one.

The Bottom line

The whole purpose of this chapter is to show you that you need to get every sale you can get.

You already spent your time getting to this home to talk to this person. You must be able to handle every situation you encounter as you go through your sales career. Do not make the mistake of saying "I don't need these kinds of people" no matter how you are treated. You need every sale you can get. Take pride in the fact that you are a professional. Several times in my career, I had customers who treated me terribly when I was talking to them regarding a product I was there to help them with. I made it my mission to get this sale no matter what they said to me. I had to have multiple sales calls with them in order to come up with the price for what they wanted. I put up with all their insults and negative comments about me and always remained respectful and friendly. However, every time I came back to this home I raised the price of the system they needed.

(My commission was based on the profit on the job) I always said, "They can treat me badly but there will be a price for them to pay".

Always be professional, whether at work or in your life.

CHAPTER 6

Making Contacts & Prospecting

I f you are going to be a salesperson, one of the first things you will need is someone to sell something to. Without this, you do not have much of a chance of being successful. If you are fortunate enough to work for a company that will provide you with qualified leads, you most likely will still have to search for new customers.

A qualified lead is one that the company has determined is pretty good before they give it to you. This means that perhaps the prospect has responded to an advertisement for your company—maybe a newspaper ad or a radio or TV commercial. The prospect could have contacted your company because of your website or maybe a mailing your company sent out. At any rate, it is a qualified lead mostly because the prospect contacted your company, and therefore it is assumed that he or she has some interest in the product you are selling. In general, these are pretty good leads.

In some cases, a telemarketing lead may be considered a qualified lead. Someone called the prospect to see if he or she had any interest in the product. If the telemarketer convinced the prospect to talk to or set up an appointment with a salesperson, then the lead is considered qualified.

The unqualified lead is a little different. This lead came in because the customer got a gift or something free just for responding to an ad or offer. In many cases, all these leads want is the free whatever and have no interest in your product at all.

Obviously, the qualified lead has a much better chance of being sold (closed) than the unqualified lead. For this reason, salespeople would rather have qualified leads.

If your company has the ability to provide you with all the qualified leads you can possibly go on or handle efficiently, then you will have no need to prospect or dig up qualified leads on your own. If, on the other hand, your company can only provide you with some qualified leads or perhaps none at all, then you must get leads on your own. This is called prospecting. The goal of prospecting is to always maintain enough leads to keep you busy handling them throughout the workweek and every workweek of the year. How do I get leads if my company is not providing me with enough of them? You make contacts and prospect.

Here is how to get started: Make a list of all the things you can possibly do to make contact with people you can talk to about your product. The things on this list should not be just the things you like to do but rather all the things you can possibly do. Start the list with the things you would most like to do and then add the things you may not like but are willing to do. Then list the things you definitely do not like to do and finally the things you will not do at all.

Your list should look something like this:
Send out mailings to people or call prospects every day that might have an interest in your product. Where you might get the names:

a. Previous customers whose sales rep is no longer with your company. These are not cold calls because you are only calling them to advise them that you will be their new sales rep. In addition, they know your company because they have done business with your company before. In the course of you advising them that you are their new sales rep, be sure to ask if you can help them with any needs for your product that they may have at this time.
b. Get a list from your service department of people that are having problems with the product they have now.
c. People whom you know are currently doing business with a competitor.
d. People you talked to in the past that did not buy from you.
e. Friends, relatives, and neighbors that might have a need for your product or service.
f. Use your existing customer base to see if they are happy and might be able to recommend you to someone.
g. A business directory or the phone book (not my favorite).

The most important thing about a plan to call or mail every day is that you must do it every day. Make a commitment to make so many calls or mailings every day and stick to it no matter what. Set a goal that you know you can live with. For example, do not say you will mail or call one hundred people a day if you know that you could never stick to it. A more realistic goal for you might be twenty-five a day. Start out with that, and if you find you can handle more every day, then increase it to thirty-five or forty. Also, if you find that you are unable to do twenty-five a day, lower it to twenty or fifteen. It does not matter how many you do. What matters is that you do it every day.

1. Stop by sites where people are using your product or have a need for your product.
2. Offer a spiff (bonus) or cash (if it is OK with your company) to people who can get you a lead that ends in a sale.
3. Attend meetings and join organizations that have people that can use your product, i.e., Rotary, Lions, homebuilder associations, senior citizens, health care associations, charitable organizations, PTA, volunteer organizations, or neighborhood associations.
4. Run for local office, e.g., school board, planning boards, zoning boards, or town boards.
5. Prospect neighbors of people that did buy from you.
6. Place your business card in all correspondence you send out. This includes all bills you pay by mail.
7. When you leave a good tip at a restaurant, be sure to leave a business card.
8. Pass out your business cards everywhere.
9. Call or send info to people who can recommend you to their customers, i.e., doctors, dentists, lawyers, architects, engineers, real estate people, barbers, hair designers, or anyone who sees many people all the time.
10. Volunteer to give speeches or seminars about your type of product at conventions or organizational meetings.
11. Offer free surveys to inspect for problems that your product will fix.
12. Go through neighborhoods and leave brochures for your company and yourself.
13. Go through neighborhoods and knock on doors to introduce your product.

See how many others you can add to the list.

14. _____

15. _____

16. _____

17. _____

Now that you have made up your list, you should pick out at least five that you either would like to do or at least would not mind doing. Start with your number one and begin working your way back to number five. In most cases, you will get more leads than you can handle well before you get to number five. If, however, you do not, just keep going down your list. I am very sure you will never have to get down to the things you will not do before you have plenty of prospects to work on and make many sales.

Remember that prospecting is like digging for gold. You have to move a lot of dirt to find the gold. However, remember to keep your focus. You are not looking for the dirt. You are looking for the gold.

CHAPTER 7

The Parts of the Sale

Preparation

The following is the roadmap to the sale. It starts where all roadmaps should start, the beginning. The beginning is really the time you receive the sales lead. This map is made up of various segments and starts with the sales lead. The most important thing you need to do is to be prepared to handle this lead.

You've Got a Lead

Great, so what are you going to do with it?

Well, the first thing you should do with it is check your schedule. Verify that the day and time of the appointment is OK with your schedule and does not present a conflict with another appointment or something else you have to do.

Next, check to see if you or someone else has sold to people in the neighborhood or other similar businesses that your prospect might know. If you are selling to businesses, this can be a real door opener for you. Obtaining information from that sale (such as the brand of equipment sold, the price, and the date of the sale) will be of great value for the call you are going on.

Before You Head Out on the Call

Make sure of several things before you head out on your call:

- Your car is clean and in good running order.
- You have all the paperwork needed to complete the sale.
- You have all the literature you will need for this call.
- Look in the mirror to make sure your appearance is acceptable.
- Make sure you have breath mints with you.
- Know where you are going and allow plenty of time to get there.
- Check on the correct pronunciation of the prospect's name or business name.

Showing Up at the Home or Business

Before it is time to show up at the home or business, be sure you check to see exactly where the home or office is so you do not spend time looking for it when you get there. A hand-held or car-type navigation system would be worth much more than they cost when you consider the amount of time saved finding where you need to go and how to get there.

You must be exactly on time for this call. If you show up early, you are not on time; it is just as if you were late.

If you are going to be late for this call by 5 or 10 minutes because of any circumstances, you must call the prospect and apologize to no end for being late. Usually the prospect could not care less that you are five or ten minutes late but will appreciate your call and will realize that his or her time is important to you.

When you do show up at the home or office, you should wait until the exact time the appointment was scheduled and then ring the bell or knock on the door at precisely that time. You see, you need to play this game. The game is this: When the prospect answers the door, step back several feet to give the prospect some space between you and him or her. If he or she looks at the watch or clock, you win the game and possibly the sale right at that point. You see, your competitors will most likely not be on time.

(If you are going to be higher on the price, you had better be different).

(Like showing up on time)

By showing up at the appointment exactly on time, this is you first case of being different. You will need to make many more cases of being different depending on how much higher on price you will be.

I say this because I never had the luxury of a low price. Every company I worked for provided the best products and service and therefore I was never able to have the lowest price for my products.

Competitors may show up early or late. In some cases, very late or maybe even not at all. By you being exactly on time, you have shown the prospect that his or her time is important to you. Therefore, after you have won the game and the prospect has looked at their watch or clock. Now you say:

Hi, I am (your first name) from XYZ Company. I have an appointment with Mr. (or Ms) _____ (their last name)

(It is **imperative** that you pronounce his or her name correctly without struggling with it. Practice saying the name before you arrive at the house or office.)

He or she will say in many cases, "You certainly are punctual," and you reply, "Well, sir/mam, I know your time is important, and I will not be wasting any of it."

Smile often and give the prospect your business card.

Remove your shoes or put on booties (only in a home, not an office).

Your Approach & Opening

Now you are ready to start your opening.

When you first get in the home or office, the prospect may try to tell you about their reason for having you there or show you what their problem is. Do not let this happen. You say, "Well, if you don't mind, I need to ask a few important questions with regard to your home first. Is there a place we could sit down and talk"?

Building Rapport

After you have settled in a good place for both of you, ask the prospect, "What was it that prompted you to invite me into your home?" Then listen very carefully to the answer. Use what the prospect says at this time regarding the reason they called and use it when it comes time to close (this solves all the concerns you called us about). At some point, you must pay them a sincere compliment. This means that it has to be a compliment that you truly believe. Look around you and find something unique to this person such as:

- A great car
- A beautiful home
- A hobby that the prospect has
- A great picture or object
- An unusually nice room or fireplace

After you have paid them a sincere compliment, continue to build rapport. Make the prospect feel important. Remember, its human nature for people to be more interested in themselves than in you or what you are telling them.

- Set the mood. Keep it light. Smile.
- Look at the person who is talking.
- Look at the prospect when you are talking.
- Listen to what they say intently.
- Let them know that you agree by nodding your head.
- Do not ever interrupt them.
- Do not ever argue with them (win the argument, loose the sale).

Then you say, "To make sure I don't miss anything and to save us some time, I have a few questions I need to ask, if you don't mind."

Make sure, (if you can) that all decision makers are present. You say, "Would there be anyone else interested in the installation of the new system?" (Or service we provide or anything else you are selling).

Now proceed with the questions on a survey analysis that you have prepared, which you customized to obtain information you will need to sell your product or service. You might want to call this a confidential questionnaire.

Some things you might want to include on your questioner:

1. When had you planned on doing this project?
2. How much have you budgeted for the project?
3. Do you have any special concerns that will need to be addressed?
4. Have you used our company in the past?
5. Will you require financing help with this?

Add some questions yourself that will apply to your product or service.

Keep it light. Smile. Remember, you are asking questions to get answers you can use to help close the sale. *You must pay attention to the answers* you can use to help close the sale. *You must pay attention to the answers* or do not bother asking the questions. If they say, they are interested in financing, you say, "We have a fine financing plan. Some plans involve no interest at all." (In some cases, you may even want to get them preapproved.)

Start the Home or Business Analysis
Set a level of expectation. Let the prospects know what you are doing and why. This helps remove any anxiety they may have about you being there.

Ask the prospects, "Have you ever had an analysis done on your home or business before?" (If they say yes, it most likely means they have gotten other bids for the job. Well, let me explain why it is important. Explain that the information from the analysis is used to determine the size and operating cost of a system.

(Service or product you are selling)

Explain something technical about your product or service that requires this information. When it is time to purchase a (car, stereo, refrigerator, or anything else), you have many options. Let me review them with you now so you may think about them while we do our survey.

You say, "Thanks for helping me with those questions. I need to gather some visual information about your home (or office). Would you mind helping me measure?" (Encourage involvement.) This step is only used if the product or service requires it, such as:

- Heating or cooling systems
- Replacement windows
- Kitchens and baths
- Additions
- Entertainment systems
- Furniture (if design and placement is included)
- Patios and decks
- Awnings

You just figure out if this step would be helpful for your product.

Survey the Home, Office, or Job Site
Get the prospect to go with you (if you can).

Note: If you must open any room doors or closet doors, you must ask the prospect if you may *before* you open it. Do this for every closet or door you must open.

- Check all areas that will involve your product.
- Measure and sketch out the layout of the home.

- Take the pictures you will need.
- Document all information required on your install survey sheet.
- Check for dirt or dust that may affect the operation of your product.

During this time, be genuinely interested in the prospect. Get the prospect to talk! Get to know him or her. Develop a relationship. Talk about:

- Family
- Occupation
- Recreation
- Material possessions
- Hobbies
- Accomplishments
- Things they are proud of

When you look at the system or product they currently have, ask questions that may lead up to selling extras. "Who in the home has needs that relate to _____(your product or service)?"

If they say that someone does, then ask. "If in the course of designing your new system I can help solve that concern, would you be interested?"

If the prospect says yes, make a note and go on. Do not try to sell it at this point. If the prospect says no, ask the same question as before.

Do not keep asking the same "If in the course of…" question. It gets old fast. Just say, "Do you want that fixed?" or something like that. Use your common sense and imagination.

- Does the current product or service provide for all your needs?
- What do you like about what you have now?
- What don't you like about what you have now?

Use these answers later to show how your product or service will provide for everything he or she likes about what they have now. It also will correct anything they do not like about what they have now.

Take four pictures of the existing product or system from different angles. (This not only is helpful to the install department but also is a major portion of "The Show.") Fill out your install survey sheet completely.

As you go through the home or job site and the prospects says they want something changed or added to a system, say, "Let me make a note of that," and address it during the presentation. If they want something done that you cannot do or would not be good for the prospect, this is not the time to address it. Make a note of it and address it at the presentation part of the call.

For example, if the prospect says they want two windows added to a room and it cannot be done, just say, "Let me make a note of that," and during your presentation say, "Now, as to your request for two windows in the family room, I have determined that this will not solve your problem. Rather, I would increase the size of an existing window in that room, and I will guarantee your satisfaction with the room."

This is also true with other equipment or products. Explain why this will be necessary and guarantee the results (if you are sure it will fix the problem).

You say, "I should have enough information to do my analysis. Let's put together some options for you."

Figure the Job

There is always a lag or let down when you start to figure the job. Do not let this be the dead spot in your interview. Have the prospect look at a third- party review book while you figure the price based on the options they said they wanted and the things you said they needed. A review book is a book made of letters and pictures from other satisfied customers that have your product or service.

- Calculate the size or style of the equipment or product you are going to propose.
- Calculate the operating cost and figure the payback if there is one.
- Calculate the price at which you want to sell the job.

Explain the true cost: The true total investment: "Most people think that when it comes to getting a new _____ (your product or service), the cost of the equipment is the total cost you pay. *Not true.* The total cost is how much the equipment costs over the length of time you plan to use it. A poor decision now could cost you for as long as you can put up with it."

Your Presentation

It is finally time for your presentation.

Pick up your presentation book and start to flip through the pages, describing each as you go along. They should include the following:

- Are you familiar with XYZ Company?
- The value of XYZ Company?

- Our _____license. (Insert any licenses you may have.)
- Our insurance certificate
- The Better Business Bureau
- Warranties that you have
- 100 percent satisfaction guarantee (If you have one)
- Good Housekeeping Seal of Approval

Show them the sales department mission statement. Every sales department should have its own mission statement apart from the company's mission statement. It should look something like this:

XYZ Company Sales Department Mission Statement
We the salespeople of XYZ Company pledge to be honest and helpful to our customers. To always look out for their best interest and to provide products and services of the highest quality to assure their comfort and safety. We will do this in a manner that no other company can provide. We will assure that after our customers purchase our products and services, they are better off than before we met them.
To this, we swear.

Signed _____
Sales Consultant

If your company does not have a mission statement or maybe does not want one (a big mistake), you can provide your own and use it yourself.

Try it; it works.

The Reasons People Buy

Before you start selling, you should know and think about the reasons people buy products and services.

1. To make money
2. To save money
3. To save time
4. To avoid or reduce effort
5. To gain comfort
6. To achieve cleanliness
7. To improve health
8. To escape pain
9. To be popular
10. To attract the opposite sex
11. To gain praise
12. To conserve material possessions
13. To increase enjoyment
14. To satisfy curiosity
15. To protect themselves or family
16. To be in style
17. To satisfy appetite
18. To impress others
19. To have beautiful things
20. To avoid criticism
21. To take advantage of opportunities
22. To be individuals
23. To protect reputation
24. To be safe
25. To solve a problem
26. To look good
27. To be able to brag
28. To look smart
29. To have more freedom
30. To keep from being bored

Remember that decisions are made on emotions but must have some logical reason to go ahead to completion. Notice I said *some*. In many cases, the logical reason to go ahead seems very illogical to us. We really do not care if it is illogical to us. The important thing is that it is logical to the prospect. Create the emotion and then provide any logical reasons to go ahead.

Emotional reasons to buy:

- Comfort and relaxation
- Entertainment
- Friends and neighbors will be jealous
- Ability to relax after work
- Driving pleasure instead of frustration
- Comfortable ride
- Children will be happier
- Good night's sleep
- Peace of mind
- More time for fun
- Pleasant looking
- Improve self-esteem
- Better image
- Look successful
- Show taste and style

Logical reasons to buy:

- Safety and security
- Spend less money on vacations
- Prices will never be lower
- Increased resale value of the home
- Lower maintenance costs

- Cheaper to operate
- Will fit better in the garage
- Six months free financing
- Excellent resale value
- Rebates on now
- Save time
- More convenient
- Better warranty
- Less physical labor
- Less legal and liability problems
- Lower medical costs

Select the ones that apply to your product or service and use them in every presentation. As you go through your presentation and spend time with the prospect, remember that people buy on emotions and try to justify it logically. Work on their emotions and give them logical reasons to go ahead now. You must build excitement at this point. Remember that excitement is contagious. The more excited you are, the more excited they will be. As you go through your presentation, use glamourous words such as *great, wonderful, fantastic, unbelievable*, and so forth.

Paint a picture in their mind of how great it will be if they have your product.

Avoid "terror words" such as:	Use instead:
Contract	Agreement
Sign (never)	Authorize
Rip out or tear out	Redesign or modify
Deposit (I hate this one)	Advance
Buy	Own
Deal (I hate this one the most)	Opportunity
Problem	Challenge

Other bids	Competitive quotes
Price	Investment

It is **imperative** that you not use these words. Put a jar in your office or home and fine yourself every time you use one of these words. Make it a habit in all conversations to never use these words. Consider them swear words.

Try it; it works.

Create desire and build rapport.

- Let prospects know you make their lives better.
- Let prospects physically see their problems.
- Show photographs of work you have done.
- Explain what you have done for others.
- Explain your warranties.
- Find a common interest.
- Use analogies.
- Let prospects know you provide one-of-a-kind products or services.
- Limit the use of *I* and *me*. Focus on *you* and *your.*
- Whatever they want done is "no problem"; we are the experts.
- Show courtesy and consideration and smile a lot.
- Use third-party stories.

Until value has been established, the price is always too high

Create Value
Wrap your value message around what is important to the prospect.

- This system will provide the energy savings you said you wanted.
- This will improve your cash flow situation.
- This product provides the dependability you wanted.
- The secret is to provide higher value, not a lower price.
- Show hard evidence of the value you are providing.
- A leading consumer magazine says this is the best.
- Here is what our customers say about us.
- As you can see, this product is the highest quality.
- Explain that you accept full responsibility for the product or service. Most people fear making the wrong decision when buying _____ (insert your product or service).
- In your proposal, spell out everything you will do. (This will also help install know what needs to be done.)
- Review company history.
- Explain exactly what they can expect regarding the installation or delivery process.
- Stress the benefits of the unit they said they wanted: lower operating costs, quiet operation, more comfortable, less maintenance, and more reliability.

You *must* mention all the features of your product but never forget:

You must never mention a feature without a corresponding benefit.

FEATURE	BENEFIT
Navigation system	Never get lost again
Antilock brakes	Less likely to get in an accident
Roller-glide shelves	Much easier to get things out
Thermo-pane glass	Lower energy costs
One million mega pixels	Better picture
Special motor	More reliability
Teflon-coated	Less maintenance
Compact design	Fits better in small places
Fully insulated	Less noise or chance of fire
Safety guard	Less chance of injury

People do not care about features. They care about what the feature will do for them. Do not make the mistake of assuming that they will know the benefit if you tell them the feature. Even if they do, they will not see how it will help them unless you tell them. I have seen salespeople go on and on about technical features that the prospect did not understand or could not have cared less about even if he or she did.

Always stress benefits, not features.

Try it; it works.

Your Product Knowledge

Many salespeople go on and on about their knowledge of the products that they sell or the items they service. Product knowledge is important if you want to select the right product for this prospect. However, remember that in a sales situation, it is a tool to the sale. It is not a badge to be worn or a way to show the prospect that you are smart and they are stupid. Use your product knowledge only as necessary to show the prospect that you are the most qualified person to get them the product or service they need or want. I like to call it *quiet confidence.* Some prospects have many technical questions that must be answered before they will go ahead. You must be able to answer them or they will lose confidence in your ability to help them. If you *cannot* answer a question, tell them that you will find that out and get back to them on a specified date and time with the correct answer. If, however, the question is not pivotal to the sale, you simply tell them that it can be addressed on installation or delivery, continue with your selling process, and get the order without answering their question at this time. If, on the other hand, the question is pivotal to the sale, and by that, I mean that the prospect will not buy until the question is answered to his or her satisfaction, then you may call someone or ask someone to stop by your location to help you answer it.

Get the Order Now

You see that I have always wanted to get the order while I was at the home or office. Remember the saying "the be back, will be back, unless he meets a salesman." If you do not get the order now or if the prospect said, he or she will be back or you can come back and get the order later, the prospect might meet a competitor that is a better salesperson than you are, in which case the prospect will buy the product or service from the other salesperson. In addition, I do not want to go back unless I have to. The most important thing I have as a salesperson is my time. If it takes two hours to make a sale and I can only work ten hours a day, then without office time I am limited to four sales a day if I close every one of them. I cannot afford to keep going back to the prospect's home or business without putting a limit on my income. What you will have to do is gamble.

Yes, you are going to have to bet that the time you spend with the prospect will result in a sale right now. When and if you determine that it will not, you must get out of there as soon as possible without killing the possibility of getting the sale later. This is not always an easy thing to do. You could bet wrong and lose a sale. If, for example, you are talking to a couple who seems to like your company, your product, and you but just does not want to go ahead now, you could bet that you will get the order at a later time and leave. If you bet wrong, the couple will buy from someone else before you get back to them. Instead, you might have bet that if you just stayed there thirty minutes longer, you would have gotten the order, and you very well might have. You must decide in this case how much time you will bet. Do you need to stay there two more hours and talk about their fishing trips in order to endear them enough to you so they will go ahead with the order? Alternatively, will you stay two or three hours and still end up empty handed. You might also look at it another way. If you spend four hours getting the order, is your commission high enough to justify the time expenditure even if you get the order? In other words, would you have been better off leaving that home or office without the order and going on to another appointment or two and selling one or maybe both of them? The only way you can make decisions correctly most of the time is by learning it from someone who knows or by learning from your own experience gained from sales call after sales call. Remember that the more sales calls you go on, the better you will get.

This is only true if you have other appointments to go on. In the event that you have no other appointments to go on for that day, then your decision to stay or go is made much easier. If you conclude that it will take another hour or two to close the sale, then it is a no brainer to decide to stay and get the order.

You will see in the rest of this book that I provide you all the information to get the order now. Please keep in mind that in general, most sales are **not** made on the first call. I always liked to try to get the order now anyway. Some companies and some products you may sell will not lend themselves easily to this process. Some products require weeks or months of calculations and sub contractors' prices before you can even come up with a price for your product or service. In this case, you can take all the steps necessary to build rapport and prospect confidence listed above, but this is not the time to try to close the sale.

What It Takes to Work for XYZ Company

Another way to build value instead of lowering the price is to build up your company. Tell the prospect what it takes to work for your company.

- Drug-free installers
- Background check required
- Driving record checked

It is a fact that we have to interview ten installers to find just two that we can hire because the other eight cannot pass our stringent drug test or extensive background check. I can personally guarantee you that some of these people are now or will soon be working for one of our competitors. Do you want to take the chance that one of these people will end up in your home with your family?

- We provide extensive training.
- We adhere to one of the toughest ethics policies in the country.

Does this sound like the kind of company with which you would like to do business? (Create doubt in doing business with other companies. However, this applies only if they have said they were getting other bids.)

Make it look as if you are not in a presentation. Keep it light and interject stories or remarks about things other than the heating/cooling system or what ever your product may be.

- People do not want to look at a presentation book.
- They will look at a book that gives them options.
- Show your price book and present the unit that you picked for them based on their wants and the requirements of the home.
- Tell the prospect that the most important day of their systems future is the day it is installed.
- Installed right = many trouble-free years of operation.

- Installed wrong = many years of trouble and wondering how you chose the wrong company (only if other bids).

Get the prospect to say, "You get what you _____ for."

Use the Sales Tools at Your Disposal

- You (what you can do for them that no one else can)
- Your company (reputation/size/service)
- Your manager (have prospect talk to the manager)
- The parent company or owner
- Your products
- Visual aides
- Product demonstration
- Testimonials
- Your success
- Your customers
- Your family (number and age of kids, your spouse)
- Your background
- Your voice inflections
- Your memberships (Rotary, Lions, Masons, etc.)
- Your hobbies
- Your product knowledge
- Your training
- Stories
- Similar hardships—use sympathy
  - (sympathy = You understand how the prospect feels)
  - (empathy = You feel as the prospect feels)
- Reports and studies
- Magazine articles
- Trade publications

- Financing
- Terms
- Survey of needs
- Special promotions
- Rebates
- Factory tours (that you have been on)
- You own the product yourself
- Your business cards
- Your goals and dreams
- Your price (you're proud of it)
- Your closing skills
- Advertisements
- Your design and application skills
- Your price book
- Your experience
- Your install department
- Where the company is located
- Licenses we have
- Certificates you have received
- Awards you have received
- Your military experience

Now add some of your own:

_____

_____

Remember, when a service tech goes into the home, he does not bring inside all the tools he has on the truck. He selects the ones he needs to get started. You will not be using all the tools listed above but only the ones necessary to get the job done. If you select the tools properly, you will be successful at the job you are there to do.

Go for the Sale

At this point, you need to make a recommendation as to what they should have. Base this on several things.

- What they said they wanted
- What you said they needed
- Their budget as you discussed it
- Your impression as to how they reacted to the top-of-the-line stuff
- Most important, what is in their best interest?

Prospects expect you to make a recommendation that fits their needs because you are an expert in your field. If you give them equipment options, it opens the door for them to say they want to think about it. Most people have trouble making decisions, as they are afraid of making the wrong one. The easiest decision is always no decision at all. Do not give them a chance to use this excuse. Instead, tell them, "Based on all the information I have collected from your home and the questions I asked you that you were kind enough to answer, here is what you should have." Go over the product or service you have selected for them. Tell them that this product or service was specifically designed for them with their needs, wants, and lifestyle in mind.

Remember, while you are telling them about the product you designed for them, do not knock other products that you have available for them because they may say the product you designed for them is the wrong one. You can always go back and design another system if the need arises. In other words, recommend the system you chose but leave the door open for other options. Then give them the price. First, go over everything that will be included. Then say, "The total investment for all this will be only $$$$$$."

Explain exactly how the job will be done.

The Close (How Do I Get The Order).

There are several kinds of closes listed below.

The Alternative of Choice
Now that we have determined this is the best equipment for your needs, I guess there is only one question we need to answer. Should we install it next Wednesday, or is another date more convenient?

The Assumption Close
Since we have taken care of all your needs in this proposal, I will just need your approval here to go ahead and schedule the work to be done.

The Do-Nothing Close
Just write the order and give it to the prospect to approve.

The Third-Party Close
Call the manager for authorization to go ahead. Call the wife/husband or advisor for final approval.

The "Have I Got a Deal For You" Close

- I have one discount coupon left.
- If you go ahead today, I have been authorized to give you a $100.00 rebate.
- If you decide to go ahead today, I think I can get you a rebate that actually ended last week.
- We have a few more gift certificates left. If you want to schedule this today, I can give you one of them.

The Summary Close

Review all the benefits the prospect said he or she wanted and needed. Then say, "That pretty much takes care of all the concerns and solves all the problems you called us about, doesn't it, Mr. Jones?" (If he says yes, write the order and ask him to approve it.) Alternatively, you could say, "Well, Mr. Jones, that pretty much covers all the concerns you had, doesn't it? Well then, let's get this thing going now, OK?"

The Customer-Closes-Himself Close (My Favorite)

Prospect says:

- We will not be available until the twelfth for installation.
- I need to get started on this right away.
- I will be out of town until the twenty-first.
- I cannot pay until the fifteenth of the month.
- Show me where the unit will go.
- Do we have to be home all day when you install it?
- Can the dog be here alone when you install it?
- We both work all day.

- My nephew will be visiting from out of town all next week.
- I do not think the old unit will last much longer.
- Do you take personal checks?
- Can I use my credit card?
- When is the soonest you could install it?

OK, now for you people who are new at this, these types of questions mean that you have sold this prospect. Yes, the job is sold. Do not go any further trying to close. Just answer their question and ask them for an install date.

The Similar Situation Close

- Most people who get a system such as this one have it installed in about seven days. Would that be OK with you?
- Other people in your neighborhood have purchased this model. Would this be the one you want to go with?
- We install more of these systems than any other company does. Does this sound like the system you want?

The Ben Franklin Close

As the story goes, when Ben Franklin had a decision he had to make, he would list all the reasons for going ahead with a project on one side of a piece of paper and all the reasons to not go ahead on the other side of the paper. This has turned out to be a classic way to close a sale. Here is how it works: When your prospects balks at going ahead now, you tell them that a good way to help make a good decision is to list all the reasons to go ahead on this sheet of paper. I will help you. Let's start with:

- Energy savings
- Comfort

- Safety
- Security
- Peace of mind
- Entertaining
- Fewer repair bills
- First-year clean and check
- Six months no interest/no payments
- Rebates
- Gift certificate
- Health reasons
- Never a better time to buy than now
- Anything else you can think of to put on the list based on needs and wants.

Be sure to help them come up with as many reasons as possible to go ahead as you can.

Now list all the reasons not to go ahead that you can think of. Make sure you do not help him or her with this part.

When the list is done, there should be many more reasons to go ahead than not. At this point, you say, "Well, that pretty much settles that, doesn't it? Shall we go ahead and get the paperwork started?"

If you can only retain one thing from this book, let it be this:

<u>Ask a closing question and then...</u>

**shut up-shut up-shut up-shut up-shut up-shut up
shut up-shut up-shut up**

If used throughout your sales career, this one piece
of information can make you more money than
any other single thing you will ever learn.

Do not ask me why this works. I learned this in a sales seminar forty years ago. Every time I use it, I am amazed at how well it works.

Here is how it goes down:

1. First, you ask a closing question. "Can we go ahead with this now?"
2. You shut up.
3. They look at each other or the prospect just thinks a while.
   The wife says, "What do you think, honey?"
   He says, "I don't know; it is very expensive."
   She says, "I know. Maybe we had better wait until next year."
   You still shut up.
   He says, "But it would be nice to have it for our daughter's wedding next month."
   She says that you did offer a great finance package for them.
   He says, "Yeah, and we pay no interest for six months. I will get my bonus check by then, and we can pay it off."
   It seems to you as if hours have passed. You begin to feel very uncomfortable. Time drags on. It seems like forever. You begin to sweat.
   Finally, they say OK, let's do it.
4. You re-enforce their decision by saying, "Down the road, you will be very glad you did this now." Write up the order.

Let's say that they were not as cooperative as you had hoped and break the conversation by saying, "Yeah, it's a lot of money, so we will wait a while before getting it."

You say, "Well, I can understand why you would say that. However, if you wait, the price will only go up. Maybe I can arrange to get you better terms on the financing if you see your way clear to go ahead now. Would that be OK?"

Now, in case you did not recognize it, this is another closing question. So what are you going to do? If you said shut up, you are right. If you said anything else, you are not paying attention to what I am trying to do here. Get with the program and shut up. When the prospects speak *to you* is when the game is temporarily over. Remember, you must shut up until the prospect speaks to you, not to someone else.

What if the prospect asks a question after you asked a closing question? Then you answer the question as simply as possible and ask another closing question. For example, you say, "Can we go ahead with this now?" and the prospect says, "Can you install it on Friday?" You *do not* say yes. You want a commitment to go ahead. You say, "Do you want it Friday?" If the prospect says yes, tell him or her it will be your pleasure to have it installed Friday, and you write the agreement.

If the question the prospect asks is more complicated, you take all the time you need to answer the question if you can or call someone to get the answer if you cannot answer it. Answer the question and ask another closing question. Example: The prospect says, "How many RPMs does this product develop?" You say two thousand, which will be plenty for your needs. Do not go into a long, technical dissertation about the motor. You already did a great presentation for the product. Now you say, "Does that answer your concerns about the motor?" (This is not a closing question.) He or she says, "Yes, it does." You now ask another closing question and shut up. "So can we go ahead with it now?" Shut up until he or she speaks to you.

You can only do this two or three times before the prospects think you are trying to pressure them. Remember, you need to apply as much pressure as you can without the prospect realizing you are using any pressure at all. This means that as far as the prospect is concerned, you must be using no pressure at all. If the prospect thinks you are pressuring him or her at all, you may very well lose the sale. You must be able to judge with this particular prospect how much pressure you may use before they think you are pressuring them. Not an easy decision for you to make at all. Only experience will let you make that decision correctly. Usually two or three closing questions are the limit. If you think you got caught using too much pressure you say, "I am not and never will be a high-pressure salesperson. I will not work for a company that requires high pressure, and I believe it is unethical."

See what their response is and proceed to leave your proposal and tell them when you will be calling them back.

However, keep in mind two things.

1. If you want to maximize your sales, there must be some pressure. Pressure on the prospect should be viewed on a scale of one to ten. You can learn from experience that you can usually get up to a five or six before the prospect feels your pressure.
2. Assuming that the product you are selling and the company you work for will make people's lives better, if the prospects do not buy this product from you, they are making a big mistake. In some cases, it could be a fatal mistake.

    Let's say you sell brakes for a company that has the best reputation for quality installation of brakes. When you tell the prospects that they need new brakes, they decide to wait until they can better afford them. If you let them walk out of your business without new brakes, they could be involved in a serious accident. If you feel this might endanger their family or themselves, then ethically you must do everything you can to be sure they buy your brakes now. Not when they can better afford it.

If the product is good for people, they are making a mistake if they do not buy it.

The main thing you need to learn about closing is that you must try to close the sale (Get the order). You should make an iron clad commitment that you will always try to close the sale (ask a closing question).

When you start out this will be hard for you to do. Nevertheless, you must ask for the order on every call you go on provided the prospect has all the information he or she needs to go ahead. If the prospect does not have all the information he needs, then you should not try to close the sale. Make another appointment to meet when you can close the sale.

Therefore, here is my expert advice to you. Before you get into all the fancy closes above, just say:

Can we go ahead with the order now?
May I go ahead with the paperwork?
Will you give me permission to schedule the job?
Remember to ask a closing question as above and SHUT UP.

If you do not learn to ask for the order, you will never be successful.

Handling Objections

OK, so all the closing techniques did not work and you **did not** get the order. You used your best closes and nothing happened.

Well, if you failed to get the order, then the prospect must have an objection. While many people think that a prospect can use many objections to avoid going ahead with the sale, in reality there are only six that will be used 95 percent of the time. Since there are only six, you may as well be prepared to handle all six of them. Below you will find what should be your standard response for all of them.

Here they are in the order you will hear them most:

I want to think it over.
Your price is too high.
I am getting other bids or quotes.
I have to talk to _____ (my wife, my father, my neighbor, etc.).
I am in no rush or no hurry.
I have no money.

In the following pages, you will learn the best way to handle each one of these. After you handle the objection, select another close (not the same one) and try it one more time.

I Want to Think It Over

First, you can be sure that this is a disguise for the real reason the prospect is not going ahead at this time. Your job is to find out the real reason. Just think a minute about the times you said you want to think about it to someone. You might have been thinking one of the following:

This person is a jerk, and I want him out of my house.
His price is so high; I just do not want to deal with him.
I really like this system, but it is just more than I can afford.

I want to go ahead with this, but I should get other bids.

I will probably go ahead with this tomorrow.

As you can see, many things could be going through the prospect's mind when they say, "I want to think it over."

Correct response: You say, "Sure, take all the time you need. This is a major decision, but just for my own information, can you tell me just what it is you want to think over?" (Do not pause here or the customer may interrupt you.) "Is there something I forgot to tell you about or did not provide enough information about?"

"Do you have some reservations about me or XYZ Company?"

"Well, OK, is there a problem with the terms?" The standard response to this question from the prospect is "What do you mean the terms?" You say, "Well, you will notice that on our agreement it says that the payment is due on completion. Does this create a problem for you?" If the prospect says yes it does, go into credit cards or special financing (six month no interest or whatever you have available). If the prospect says the terms are not a problem, you say, "OK, look, be honest with me, is it the price?" If it turns out that price is the real problem, go on to the next objection, "Your Price Is Too High."

Your Price Is Too High
This is a good type of objection. You can handle this one.

The first thing you say is "I see" and then wait for a response from the prospect. Sometimes, the prospect says, "But I want your company to do the work, so let's go ahead with it."

When you say, "I see," the prospect might reply, "Well, I am not going to pay that much." You say, "I can appreciate that. Can you tell me why you think it is too high?"

If the prospect says, "It's too high compared to what my neighbor paid," you say, "What did your neighbor get and how much did they pay?"

If the prospect says, "It's too high compared to what I thought it would be," you say, "Well, I would love to be able to sell these products at prices that people thought they would be, but I just can't. However, maybe I can help you out. How high is too high?" When he or she answers with a price, you say, "Mr. or Ms. _____, did you know that the money difference between the best car and the worst car can be as much as one hundred thousand dollars? Most people cannot afford the best. The spread is too high. However, when it comes to (whatever product or service you sell), the spread from the worst to the best is only two thousand dollars. Most people can easily afford that because this (product or service) pays for itself. So, if you can afford the best, you should have it. Don't you agree?"

If the prospect says, "It's too high compared to the other bids I have," you say, "So, if I understand you correctly, you're interested in paying the lowest price. Well, I am sure you know that the lowest price usually includes the lowest quality. I mean, I have never been able to get the highest quality product at the lowest price. Let me ask you something. If all things were equal, what company would you prefer to buy it from?" If the prospect says XYZ Company (your company), then you can be sure that he or she will pay you $200.00 to $400.00 more than anyone else will.

You cannot be arrogant about the price. When a prospect complains about the price, you need to build value as described above.

However, you need to show that you are cooperating with the prospects. If they make you an offer, you must not laugh or ridicule the prospect. You must show that you understand their concern regarding the price.

You say, "Well, Mr. Jones, I sure would like to accept your offer because it would be a win situation for all of us.

a. "You would get a great product at a below-cost price.
b. "The company would get to move out another _____ (whatever you are selling).
c. "I would make a sale. It would be great. However, I must apologize. I just cannot do it.

"On the other hand, I don't want to give you a price and say in effect take it or leave it. So if I can get you…

a. A reduction in the price of _____
b. A rebate of _____
c. A gift certificate for _____
d. A free first-year inspection

(Anything you can give no matter how small)
…will we be able to go ahead now and you can start enjoying your new _____?

Always remember that the prospects have been educated that "nobody pays retail." They need something to tell people they got a great deal. They need to be able to say they did not pay retail. Sometimes the prospect needs something from you in order to go ahead now or they will find a company that will give them some incentive to go ahead now. Get your company to let you give a prospect like this anything that will allow you to close this customer now. If they will not, quote the prospect a slightly higher price and come down in order to get the sale now.

I Am Getting Other Bids or Quotes

This one scares salespeople into reducing the quoted price more than any other objection. *That is why prospects use it.* Do not even think about reducing your price at this point. (Sometimes people say they are getting other bids but actually do not. They just need some time before they will go ahead, or they want to buy it from you but use the "other bid" objection to get you to come down on the price.)

Here is how you handle this situation. Ask the prospect, "Well, certainly you can get other quotes if you want to. However, if you don't mind, can I ask you why you are getting other quotes?"

Prospect says he wants to see some other prices.

You say, "Oh, I see. So price is the most important thing to you." In 95 percent of the cases, the prospect will say, "No, price is not the most important thing."

You say, "I'm confused. You said you were getting other quotes because you wanted other prices, but price is not the most important thing to you. If price is not the most important thing to you, then what criteria will you use to make your final decision?"

Prospect says, "Well, I want to hear what other people have to say as far as size of equipment, brands, what will be needed to do the job right."

You say, "Well Mr. _____If you get four quotes, you could get four brands, four different sizes, and four prices. I think you will be so confused that you would have a very hard time figuring out who is putting in the correct size and which brand is the best for the money. Therefore, I would suggest that at some point you would need to trust a company to do the right thing for you. If it were me, I would select the company that has over fifty years in the business, is a member of the Better Business Bureau, enjoys an excellent reputation for customer service, and will provide you with a great guarantee. Does that make sense to you?"

Prospect says yes.
You say, "Well, the only company that can provide those things is XYZ Company. So, could we go ahead with this now? Then you won't have to go through having all those other people in your home."

Remember, leaving the home with a high price on the table would not be in your best interest. If you cannot close the sale, tell the prospect that maybe the manager could do something to get him or her a better price. You will speak to the manager and call the prospects back (after they have all there other quotes). Ask them when they had planned to make a decision on this.

Remember, you must never knock the competition directly. Instead, spend most of your time saying how good we are **not** how bad they are. You can knock the competition without appearing to do so. When the prospect mentions another company, act surprised. You say, "Oh! You are getting a price from them." Then shut up and do not say anything more. If the prospects asks why you said, "Oh!" when they mentioned the other company, say, "I am very sorry, but it is company policy to not comment on that company."

This puts a lot of doubt in the prospect's mind about that company.

You can get them to show you the other bids. First, they say they can buy it from XYZ Company for $600.00 less than from you. Rest assured they are lying by at least $200.00. That means you are only $400.00 high. At any rate, ask them if the other proposals include a filter dryer. They say they do not know. Ask them to go get the other proposals and look at them to find out. They will look at them and act very confused. Ask if you may look at them to help them out. If they hand you the proposals, they will say, "Oh, I made a mistake. They are only four hundred dollars lower than you." Look over the proposals and point out what is missing. Remember that at this point if the prospect wants your company, they will pay $200.00 to $400.00 more, you are either $200.00 high or right on the money. Go ahead and close the sale. Great job.

I Have to Talk to _____
"I have to talk to _____before I can go ahead."

Insert anyone in the blank field such as *my wife, my husband, my father, my son, my neighbor,* or anyone else. It does not matter. It is obvious that they need an OK from someone in order to go ahead with the job.

You say, "Of course, I can see how you would want to do that. Can you call _____ now and discuss this with him/her while I get a few more measurements in the basement?"

Prospect says, "No, I'm sorry, but _____ will not be available until _____ p.m. tonight. I will talk to _____ then and let you know."

You say, "Well, you certainly are doing the right thing talking to _____, but if it is OK with you, I could get the paperwork out of the way now (along with the financing paperwork if applicable), and I could put in big letters on the proposals 'subject to _____ approval.' That way we can get things going now. Would that be OK?"

Prospect says, "No, I really don't want to do that."

You say, "OK, I can understand your apprehension. Why don't we do this? Let's set up another appointment when _____ can be here to ask any questions and to check the whole thing over."

Let's address the role of the advisor in our sales presentation. The most important thing about the prospect's advisor is that you show him or her huge amount of respect. You see, in many cases the prospects' have asked this person to help them with the final decision because they trust their opinion or believe the advisor knows a lot more about this type of product than they do. Your job is to win over the advisor. You must always build up the advisor in the eyes of the prospect. When the advisor asks a question about you, your product, or your company, you always say, "That's a good question." To the prospect you say, "It's a good thing you asked _____ (use his or her name) to be here today." Then be very specific in answering their question. When you have answered the question, ask the advisor, "Does that answer your question?" and get them to say yes. If the advisor makes a comment that is very wrong, you say, "Well, _____, we used to do it that way but now we use _____ (whatever is the correct answer)." The key is to never make the advisor look bad in the eyes of the prospect. If you do, you can be certain that the advisor will kill any chance you had of getting the sale.

I Am in No Rush or No Hurry

Some people call for a quote on a project long before they intend to get it done.

Sometimes they are just getting some quotes, and maybe they are not too serious about going ahead with purchasing new equipment at this time. The first thing you say to this is "how soon had you planned on doing this project?" Also at this point, be sure to ask them if they have a budget for the project so you might know what price range they would like to stay within. This will be extremely important later when you try to close and you will know if the price you can quote them will be within or close to their budget.

Try to get an answer from them as to when they intend to get it done.

Now you say "I see John (or Jane) Well, I am sure you know that many things can change as time goes by. The price for instance can change dramatically in just a few weeks. The quote I give today will only be good for thirty days. We rarely raise prices, but many things happen, such as equipment changes and labor changes. Frankly, even the weather can affect our prices. If we get busy, the price can be higher. Therefore, the best time for you to do this is now. I can call the manager and see if he (or she) has any specials that might help you want to go ahead now. Would you like me to do that?"

If money is the concern, you say, "I have six months no payments-no interest available now. That means we could go ahead and install the unit now or even one month from now with no money down, and you will not have to pay anything until six months after it is installed. In addition, if any rebates are announced before you actually have it installed, I will see that you get the rebate. Therefore, you have nothing to lose by doing it now. Shall we go ahead with it?"

I Have No Money

Again, use the financing plan above and see if that solves the problem. In some cases, the prospects may say they also have bad credit. Many salespeople bale out on the prospect at this point. In many sales-training courses, they even tell you to get out.

This is where your creativeness should be at its peak.

You say, "(Mike and Mary), is there a relative that owes you a favor or would get great pleasure from helping you out with this? Perhaps you have an anniversary or birthday coming up that would warrant a great present like central air?"

In a case where the prospect needs a new _____ anything that is imperative, you say, "(Mike and Mary), is there a good friend or relative that would help you out in this time of emergency? After all, you cannot use the _____ you have, and we sure cannot let you all get sick or be in danger. Let's give them a call and see if they will help. Maybe we could use their credit card and you could pay them back in payments. On the other hand, they could just loan you the cash. Also, this furnace would make a great gift for an anniversary or birthday."

You Did Not Get the Order

If all your attempts to close the sale fail, you can have one last shot at getting the order if you want to try it. I have always called it the *Silver Bullet*. After all attempts at getting the order have failed, you simply ask the prospects "What do I have to do to have you go ahead with this now"? If they say anything you can actually do, then say "ok" and close the sale. If they just say we are going to wait, then you need to find out from the prospects when they will be making a decision on their new system. Whatever day or date they pick, you must make an appointment to at least call them back exactly on that day and time or make another appointment to meet with them after that date. If they make you an offer that you cannot accept, then tell them you will bring that offer to the manager and let them know what he says.

You might want to leave the door open as to price in any case at this time if they are getting other quotes. You can try one of the following:

- "I will talk to the manager to see if he can do better on the price."
- "I might be able to get you a rebate."
- "We would like to have you for a customer, so I will try to get you a better price."

Now, the most important thing about saying you will do better on the price is that you do not tell the prospects how much better you will do under any circumstances. The prospects' will try everything to get you to tell them an amount. Do not give one. Just say, "I really don't know as I have nothing to say about the price." You might have to say this five times, but do not give them a figure. This way they will be unable to go ahead with anyone else until they hear how much better you can do.

If you do exactly what you have just read, then you have done everything you can to get the order without upsetting the prospect.

If you failed to get the order on this call, then ask the prospects when they are going to make a final decision on going ahead. If they say next month, you say, "That's fine. Would it be OK if I called you next month, maybe around the fifteenth?" If they say yes, then ask what would be the best time to call. Write down the day and time in your appointment book and tell them you will call at that time.

Now, pay attention. There is no way you can afford to wait until next month to call them back. Do you understand what I am saying? You cannot wait until next month to call them back. If you are dumb enough to do that, they will tell you what a great deal they got on a product just like yours only cheaper. You will lose this sale.

Therefore, you must call them back within forty-eight hours. However, you do not want to look as if you are pressuring them to go ahead.

Your call should go something like this: "Mr. Jones? This is Bob from XYZ Company. I am sorry to call you before next month, but I have some exciting news I thought you might be interested in." Now, the news can be many different things, such as:

1. There is now a rebate on the product.
2. We are having a special on the model you wanted.
3. I forgot to tell you about our five-year warranty.

Use whatever reason for calling that you think is good. However, remember that *you must call them back*. I want you to keep calling them back (but ask them if it is OK for you to call each time) until they buy from you or someone else.

Every month or so, go back over the leads you did not sell and call them to let them know you are still thinking about them.

A not-too-bright salesperson once said to me, "If they want it, they will call you." He retired early and broke.

If they want it really, really, really bad, they will call you, but if they only want it really, bad, they will wait for *you* to call *them*. Do not be a fool. Please believe me. If you don't understand or believe that you must call the prospect back until he buys or tells you to stop calling him, then do yourself a big favor and find another profession.

Now you have a manual to maximize your closing average and have gained the ability to close the job on the spot. Do not get concerned if you do not get the order. If you have done all the procedures above, then you have done a great job. Most people who buy do not buy on the first call.

Do not exert too much pressure on the customer to buy or you may risk not getting the order the next day or the next week or even maybe the next year. However, remember that you must exert some pressure at some time.

If you do exactly what you have just read, then you have done everything you can to get the order without upsetting the prospect.

CHAPTER 8

Customer Service

There are two parts to good customer service.

1. The policies your company has in place to deal with customers.
2. The people you have dealing with your customers.

Let's start with your company's policies regarding customer service. As a salesperson, many times your customers are left in the hands of your customer-service department to take care of their problems or concerns. The people in customer service may have their hands tied by company policies when it comes to helping your customer solve a problem he or she may be having.

If you were fortunate enough to work for a company with A-1 customer-service policies, they would look something like this:

1. The customer is always right.
2. Therefore, you never argue with the customer.
3. The company has some flexibility built into its warranty policy that allows some things that are not covered by the warranty to be covered for this customer.

4. Your service department will bend the policy to help solve a customer problem.
5. Your company belongs to the Better Business Bureau.
6. Your company offers a 100 percent satisfaction guarantee for a limited time.
7. The warranty on workmanship never runs out. This means that if something was installed wrong at the initial installation, it will be repaired at any time that it is discovered, no matter how long it takes before the problem is detected.
8. One person in your company is responsible to see that customer complaints are handled quickly and to the customer's satisfaction. He or she tracks all complaints and must report to a manager as to the progress being made to solve the complaint.

This type of customer service does not come cheap. However, a company that provides this type of customer service gets a reputation for taking good care of its customers and has no problem bringing in leads for you, or customers into your business. The one thing that you can be sure of, however, is that your prices will be much higher than your competition's price for the product you are selling. A salesperson who sells on price alone will not have much success working for this company.

Many companies have customer service that will not include all of the above policies. Some may have only six or five of the above eight policies. These may still be good companies, and their prices will probably be lower than a company that has all.

The companies that provide none of the above policies will have the lowest prices and will not enjoy a good reputation. They will still get lots of business. However, because they have the lowest prices, their competitors (that provide better quality products and good customer service) will have much higher overhead. Therefore, charge higher prices. Because they have higher prices they need very high quality salespeople in order to able to sell at the higher price.

That brings us to the second part of our customer-service program: the people you have that deal with your customers.

Some customer-service people you have met have no business being in that department at all. They are miserable and mean. They could not care less about the customer or their problems. They have a negative attitude. They try to find every excuse in the book not to help the customer.

Here are some things the customers will hear from your customer service people when they have problem.

1. That is not our problem. It is not covered under your warranty.
2. The person who takes care of that problem is off today.
3. You will have to come back when the manager is here.
4. You will have to take that up with the manufacturer. We did not build the product.
5. What do you expect me to do about it?
6. Don't worry about that noise; they all do that.
7. You are the only customer who ever complained about that.

I think you get the picture. These people should not be allowed to talk to your customers. They are sending them to your competition every day. With customer-service people like this, you will not have any customers left. You cannot imagine what an effect this has on your company's ability to get leads and have prospects for salespeople such as yourself.

There is one thing you can be sure of, however: The fault for this kind of customer service is not the service reps themselves. The fault lays with their boss or customer-service manager and in most cases the owner of the company. No owner or manager of this company would allow this type of customer service unless they feel the same way about their customers as the bad customer-service rep does. If you are ever treated like this at a company you bought from, in most cases I submit to you that when you ask to see the manager, you will be treated the same way. Generally, if you are treated like this at a company, it is because the manager or even the owner feels the same way.

When I teach customer service to companies, the first thing I say is that the customer-service people in the company must learn four words:

I'm sorry; you're right.

When the customer says, "You people are terrible at taking care of customers."

You say, **"I'm sorry; you're right."**

When the customer says, "I have been given a runaround trying to get this thing fixed."

You say, **"I'm sorry; you're right."**

When the customer says, "I was told this would be fixed today, and now they have to order a part."

You say, **"I'm sorry; you're right."**

Just keep saying it repeatedly, and eventually the customer will say, "I didn't mean to take this out on you; I know it isn't your fault."

You say, "Well, I am very sorry you have been treated this way. I have no excuse for your dissatisfaction, but I will take on your problem personally and do everything I can to see you get the service that all our customers deserve."

The first thing you must do to comfort your irate customer is *not* offer excuses, such as:

We have been very busy this week.
The person who handles that is out this week.
We are very short-handed.
Our customer-service department burned down last week.

You get the point. Customers only care about their problem, not yours.

Just keep apologizing to him or her and do not offer excuses. Just say you will take care of it now.

Remember: *I'm sorry; you're right.* It costs the company nothing and can save a valued customer or account.

These strategies are designed to clear pathways through your prospect's objections to going forward with products that will make him or her more comfortable, save energy and money, and keep his or her family safe. We are very fortunate that all our products and services help people in many ways.

If prospects do not buy from you, they have made a big mistake.

It is your responsibility to see that this does not happen.

CHAPTER 9

Other Good Stuff

What You Don't Say—The Things You Say Determine Your Pay

Y ou have all met salespeople that seem to make a good living but just do not say the things that get the sale. Well, what they have learned is not to say the **wrong** thing. They have mastered the art of not saying the wrong thing. That is right; you can be a halfway decent salesperson just by not saying the wrong thing.

Here are some of the *wrong* things to say:

1. If you are a man, do not ever call a woman *sugar, honey, sweetheart*, or *darling*.
2. Don't ever say, "Look, lady, this is the way we do it," (or "look, lady" anything, or just plain "*look, _____*" to anyone).
3. Don't ask anyone how old he or she is (unless required by law).
4. If anyone says, "How old do you think I am?" do not even think of answering that.
5. "Are you going to buy today?"
6. "What can I sell you today?"

7. "Do you have any money?"
8. "How is your credit?"
9. "Are you married?"
10. "Do you live alone?"

Remember to treat people, as you would like to be treated when you are looking to buy something. Always ask yourself, "Would I want someone to say that to me?"

Moving on Up

At some point in your career if you have done all the right things, you will be offered a job as manager. It might be marketing manager or department-sales manager or general-sales manager. This might sound like a great job at first, but before you jump all over this, here are a few things to think about.

1. What happened to the previous sales manager?
   a. Was he or she fired?
   b. If so, why?
   c. Will you do better than they did?
2. Are you happy doing what you are doing?
3. Will this job involve more travel?
4. Are you making more money than the manager's job pays?
5. Will you have to work more hours?
6. Will you have to relocate?
7. Do you like selling better than managing?

I was faced with this situation at one time in my career. I was hired to be the general-sales manager when I left the car business. After about five years of being sales-and-marketing manager, I saw that the top salespeople made more money than I did, worked fewer hours, and had a lot less responsibility.

I was happy at my job but wanted a change. I asked the boss if I could be a salesman, and he agreed as long as I would hire and train a new sales manager. I did and went into sales. I loved it. I became the top salesperson in my first year, and I held that title for almost every year I was in sales. I did that for eight years, and then a new company bought our company. It was very sales-motivated and wanted me to be the sales manager again. By this time, I was ready to take on some new challenges, and I took the job. It paid very well, and I could pretty much run the entire sales department as I wanted. I kept that job until I retired and enjoyed it very much.

The reason I included this part of my life is to let you know that moving up should be a tough decision for you. As a top sales-person in your company, you have great job security. This is not true as a manager. As you may well know, managers come and go. The position is much more political than a salesperson is. By that, I mean that as manager you might be shot at from all direc-tions in your company. Other salespeople may have wanted that job and may try to make you look bad. Maybe the owner's son or daughter works at the company, and he or she would like to see you gone. Many challenges might arise for a manager that a top salesperson never would face.

With that said, I will say that this could be the best thing that will ever happen in your career. This step could lead to becoming president or CEO of your company. Take your time and do what is right for you.

For me, the absolute best thing about being the sales manager was that I trained many salespeople in my life and was so proud when they became number one or number two at the company and even moved on to other companies as managers.

Things You Can Use

Here are some very good statements and questions that can stimulate the prospect's mind and get them thinking about going ahead with XYZ Company.

"If all things were equal, which company would you prefer come into your home and do this job?" If they say your company, you can be sure they will pay you more money than another company.

"When had you planned to do this project?"

"If you can afford it, you should have the best." (Then show them how they can afford it.)

"You can't get the highest quality at the lowest price, but you can get the highest quality for just a little bit more."

"Are you familiar with the new _____ and _____ (your products)?"

"If you need to trust someone to do this job with respect to the size of the equipment, safety, the model that best suits your needs, and care of your home and possessions, why not choose a company with over fifty years' experience, a membership in the Better Business Bureau, and a great satisfaction guarantee? You can't lose."

"If you were going to start saving money, when would be a good time to start?"

"What criteria will you use to make your decision?"

"The lowest price is always the worst value."

"You always get what you pay for."

"There ain't no free lunch."

"What do I have to do to go ahead with this now?" (The Silver Bullet)

Statements you should always keep in mind:

a. If you are going to be higher (price), you had better be different.
b. Until value is established, the price is always too high.
c. The "be back" will be back unless they meet a sales professional.
d. If the product will make the prospect's life better, they are making a mistake if they do not buy it.
e. Nobody pays retail.
f. Nothing happens until the sale is made.

How Did I Do?

You must analyze every sales call you go on. You cannot afford to keep going on calls and not learning something from every one of them. Make yourself a checklist to be used after each call, whether you sold it or not. Ask yourself the following:

1. Did I build rapport and get the prospect to like me?
2. Did I answer all their concerns?
3. Did I do a good job with my presentation?
4. Did I use the right sales tools?
5. Did I forget to tell them something?
   a. Financing
      (I use to always forget to offer financing. It cost me many sales.)

b. Rebates
c. Sales
d. Quick delivery

You will be a professional and a winner in life. I know this because people who keep trying to learn really care about being successful. That is why you read this book.
Robert F. Dieterich

Author Biography

Robert F. Dieterich started selling cars when he was twenty-four. Lured by an ad that said he would get a new car to use every six months, he found the career of a lifetime. Dieterich spent ten years as a car salesman, twenty-six years as a sales manager and sales rep. of a heating and cooling company, and eleven years running his own consulting business before retiring after a sales career that spanned forty-seven years.